The Cymbal Crashing Clouds

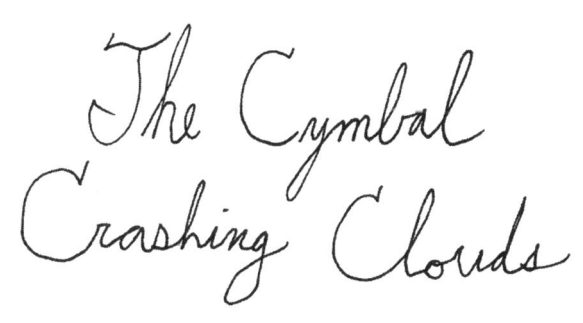

by Ben Shive

illustrated by Benji Anderson

The Cymbal Crashing Clouds © 2011 by Ben Shive
www.BenShive.com

Published by
Rabbit Room Press
523 Heather Place
Nashville, Tennessee 37204
info@rabbitroom.com

RABBIT ROOM
PRESS

All rights reserved. No portion of this book may be reproduced, stored in a retrieval system, or transmitted in any form or by any means—electronic, mechanical, photocopy, recording, scanning, or other—except for brief quotations in critical reviews or articles, without the prior written permission of the publisher.

Design by Joel Anderson
www.AndersonDesignGroup.com
Illustrations © 2011 by Benji Anderson

ISBN 978-0-9826214-5-5
Printed in the United States of America

11 12 13 14 15 — 6 5 4 3 2 1

Scripture quotations are from The Holy Bible, English Standard Version® (ESV®), copyright © 2001 by Crossway, a publishing ministry of Good News Publishers. Used by permission. All rights reserved.

The Cymbal Crashing Clouds

TABLE OF CONTENTS

Prologue

Listen!

EGBDF

Sorry But I'm Yours

Someone Is Asking

The Fall

Shooting The Moon

She's Invincible

The Fire Pit

Your Secret Smile

A Last Time For Everything

Prologue

The kid across the street and I
Shared a given name
And a seat on the bus every day;
Even the houses we lived in looked the same.

He swore a corridor was hidden behind
The walls of his house—his and mine—
And I believed him
'Cause why would he lie?

I envisioned my own private hideaway,
Silent except for the whine of the wheels in my mind,
And I came home in a fever to find it.

While he was flipping channels of cable cartoons
I was feeling for panels concealed in my room,
And back on the bus I said,
"Can I get a clue?"

He would never tell, but he stuck to his story,
And I to my search for the well-hidden door—
Kind of a gullible stay-at-home explorer.

Maybe my bookshelf would slide to the side
If I could find the lever cleverly disguised
Behind Bible-brown bindings.
So I tried a few titles and—surprise!—
I found secrets in passages lined with rhymed writing.

And I followed them deep inside of my secret heart,
To a room that was mine to hide in alone with my
thoughts.

But someone was coming. I heard breathing.
As I listened it changed to A Name, A Name repeating.
My senses awakened, awaiting the imminent meeting.
I was Adam in the garden, naked in the cool of the evening,
With nowhere to run from the Word the world was speaking.
Then a hand in the dark on the door of my heart was beating.

But my chambered heart was made for this encounter.
Every blue blood vessel had borne me to this hour.

And the room inside my heart
Was a room inside his heart.

When I came to, I knew something had changed;
I was back in my room but the colors were all strange.
So I put on a 45" to maybe clear up my head,
But instead the room spun and I went under again.

As the needle deciphered the song from the vinyl,
I went stumbling down halls ever spiraling—
~~Drawn to the center, the strings all ascending,~~
~~A long chord decaying, a song in a circle unending~~

Drawn to the center, a spirit ascending,
A body decaying—then in a world without ending I'll sing:

NEVERCOULDBEANYOTHERWAYNEVERCOULDBE
ANYOTHERWAYNEVERCOULDBEANYOTHERWAY
NEVERCOULDBEANYOTHERWAYNEVERCOULDBE
ANYOTHERWAY!

And I found it!
I finally found it!!

LISTEN!

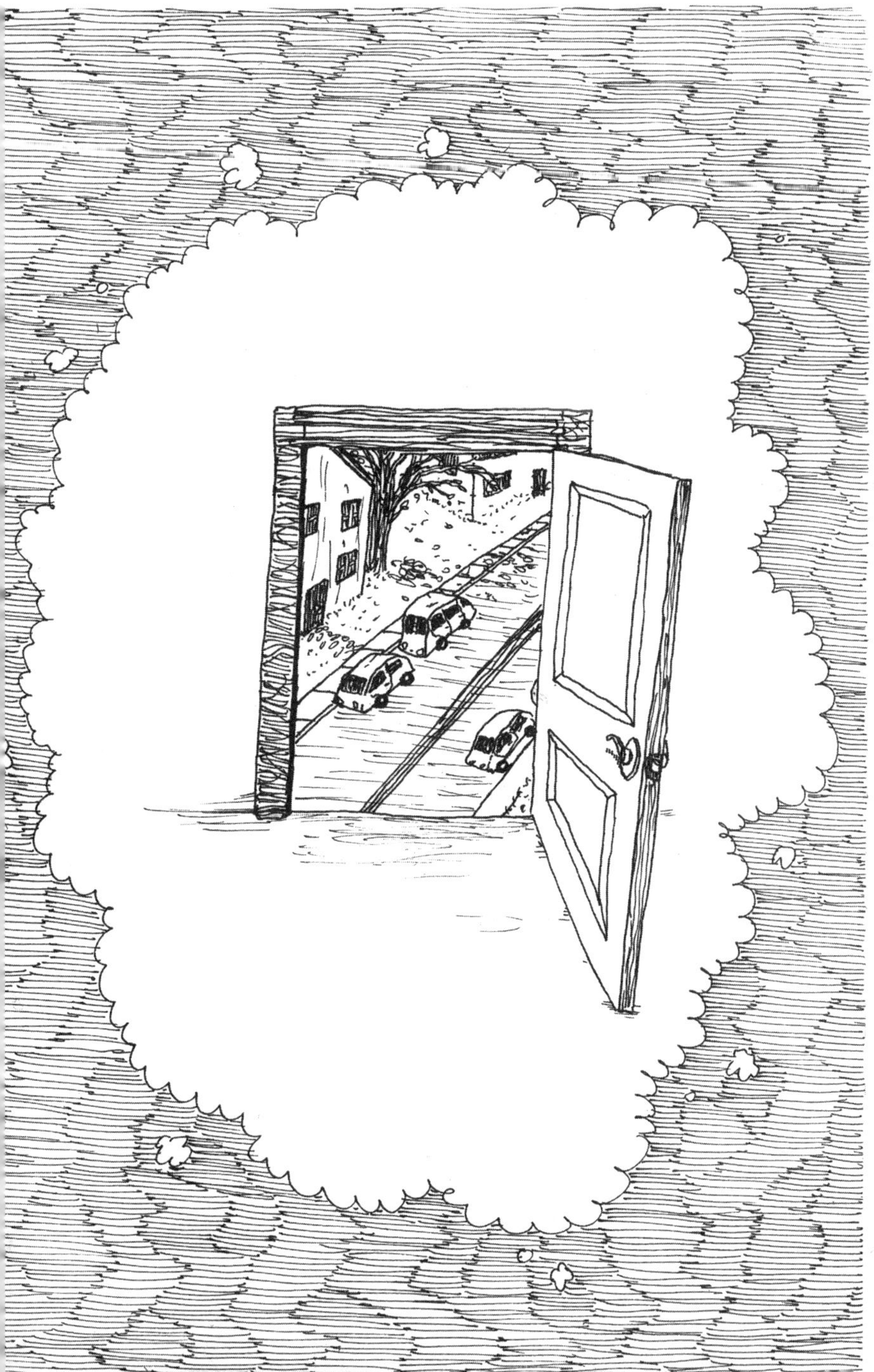

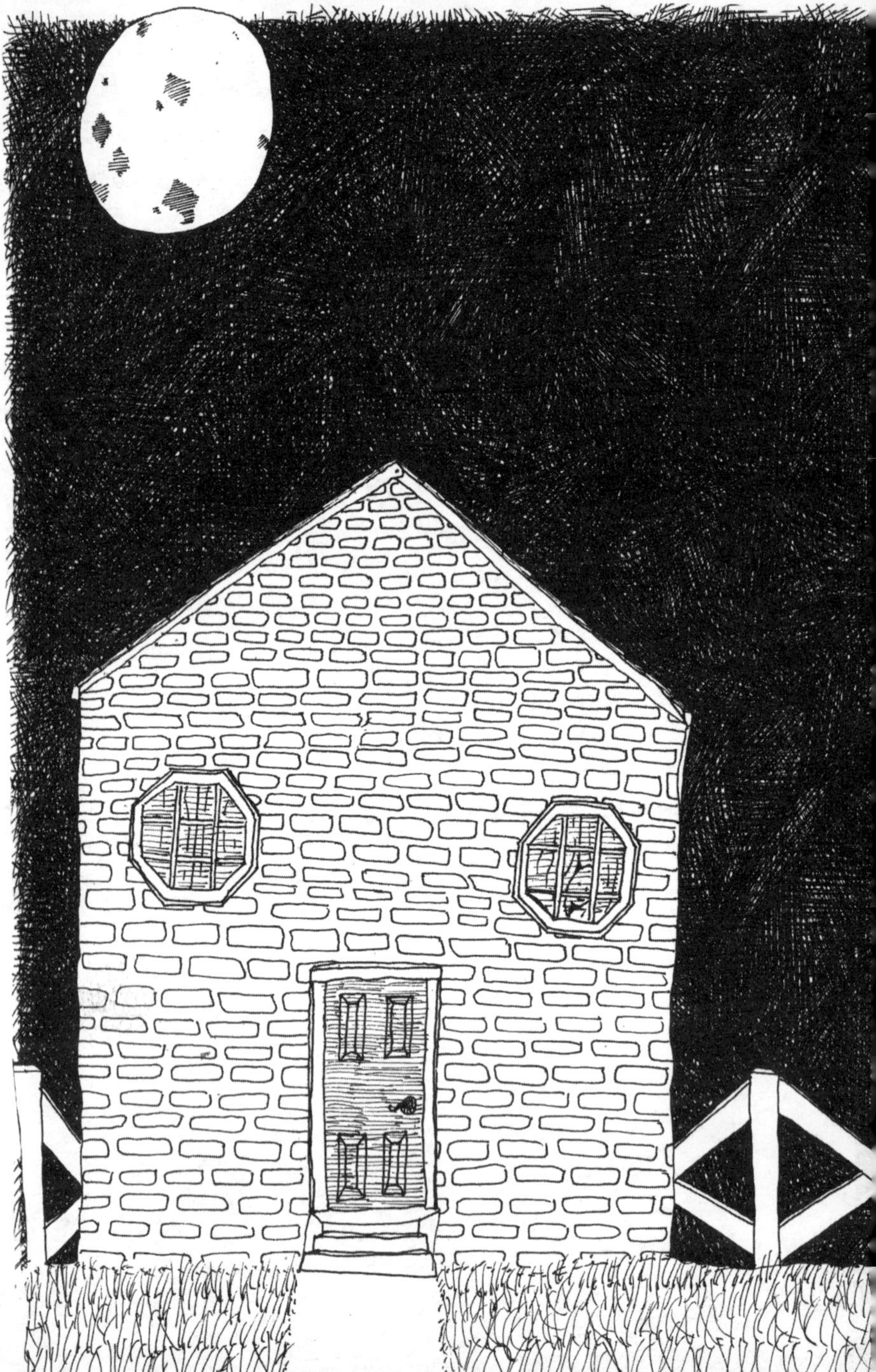

I pass through a door in a dream,
Hidden in the cleft of the night
Among the parked cars lining the street,
Robed in petals of white,
Where the seeds spin down from the trees—
Whirling angels in free flight—
And the houses mutter in their sleep,
Covered in shuttered eyes.

Listen!

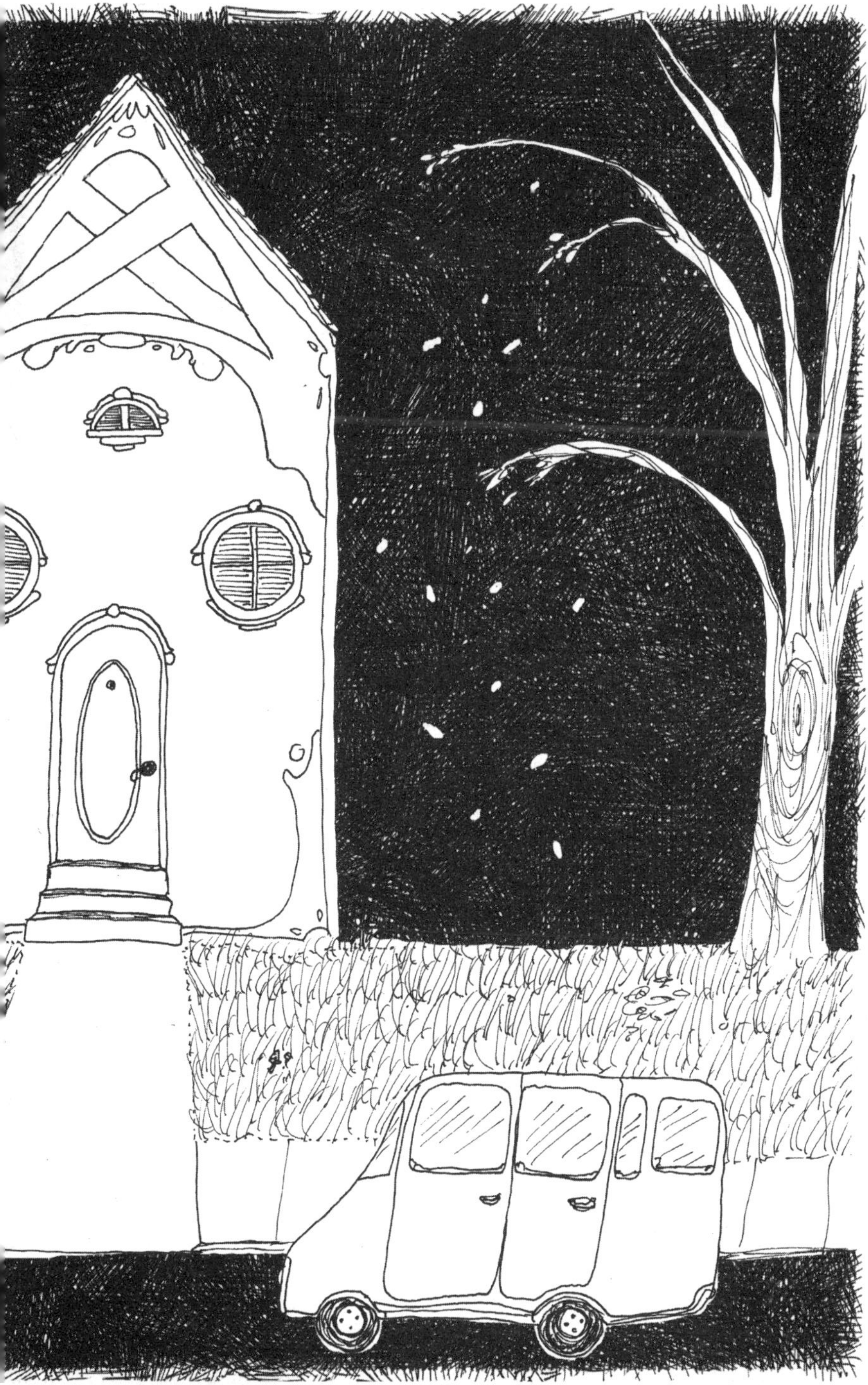

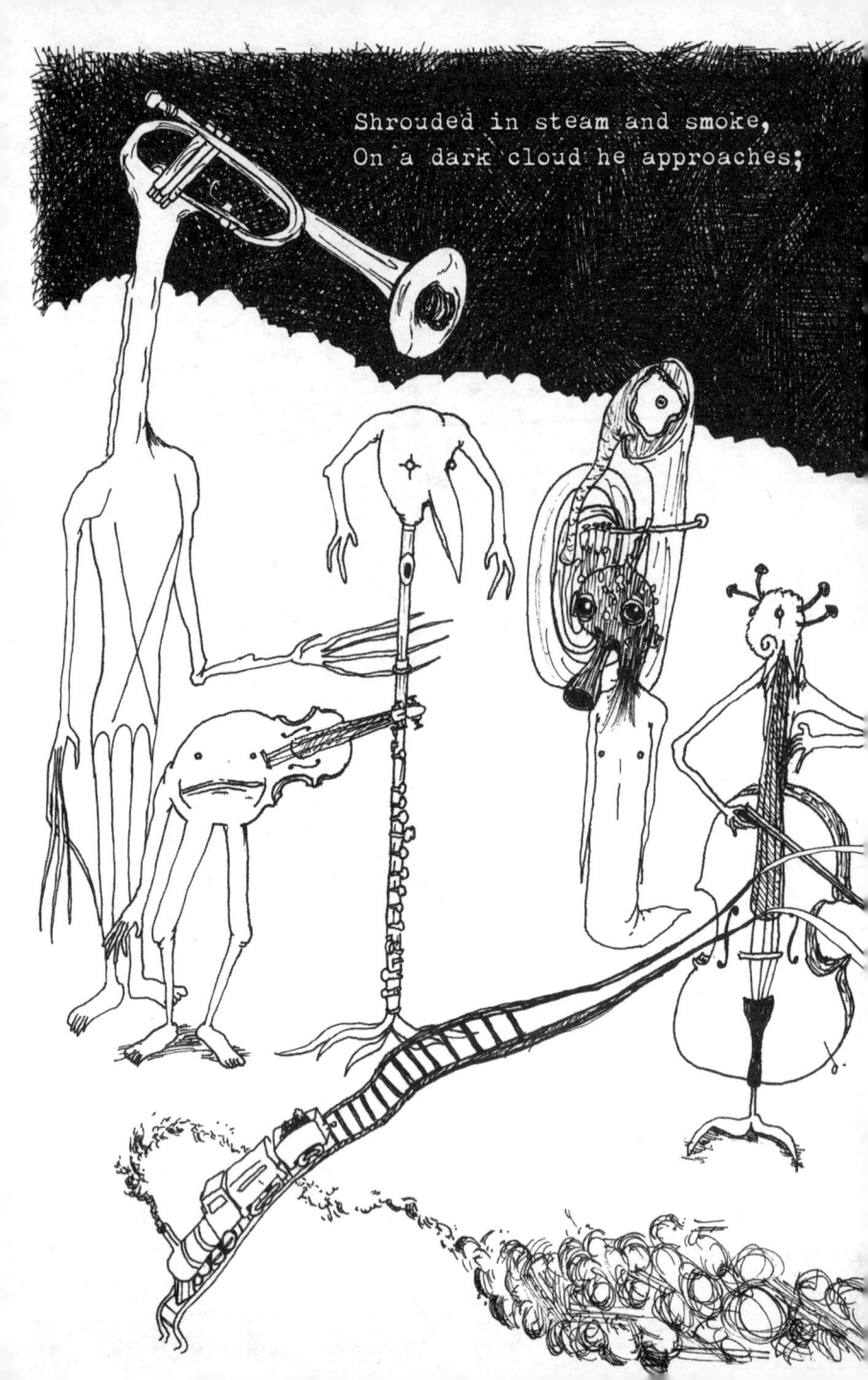

Shrouded in steam and smoke,
On a dark cloud he approaches;

And the tails of his coal-black coat
Are a train of lumbering coaches.
He passes unseen like a ghost,
But he thunders like a herd of horses.
And he calls to the heavenly host
To join with their airy voices.

Listen!

The whistle blast echoes so loud
That it rings the bell of the sky—
A song that sounds and resounds;
An unbearable, aching sigh;
Like a parliament of owls—
Silver wings brushing my eyes;
Crossing arms drawing the phrase out,
Holding the moment in time.

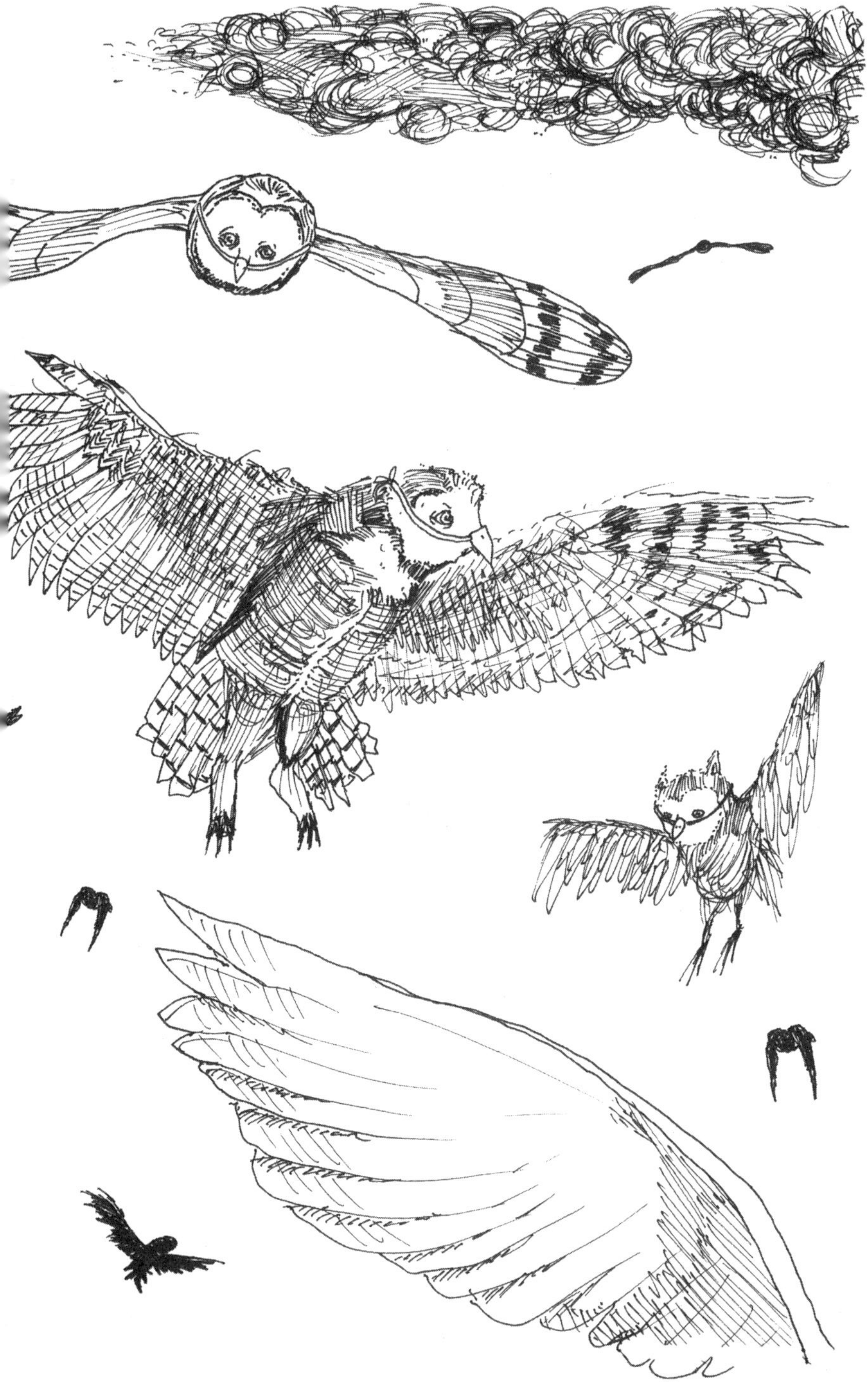

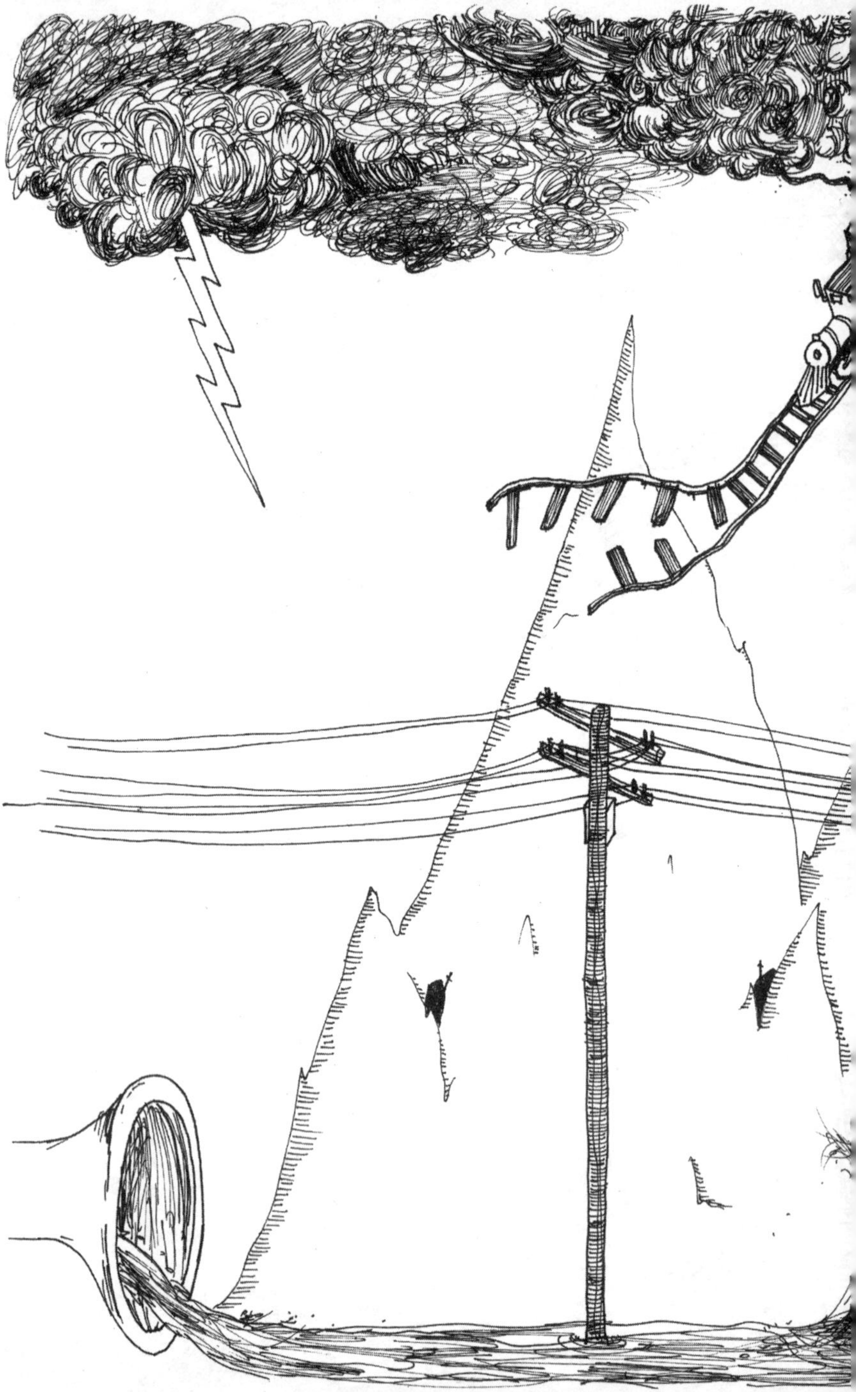

So signal the cymbal crashing clouds,
Pluck all the steeples and spires,
Cue the rivers with the reeds in their mouths,
Conduct the electrical choirs,
Rattle every window in town,
Strum all the telephone wires,
Crossing arms drawing the phrase out...

'Cause my bones are all bells to be rung;
My nerves are attuned and tight.
So come knock the air from my lungs
Out over the cords in my windpipe.
My skin pulled taut like a drum,
I am bracing myself for the strike.

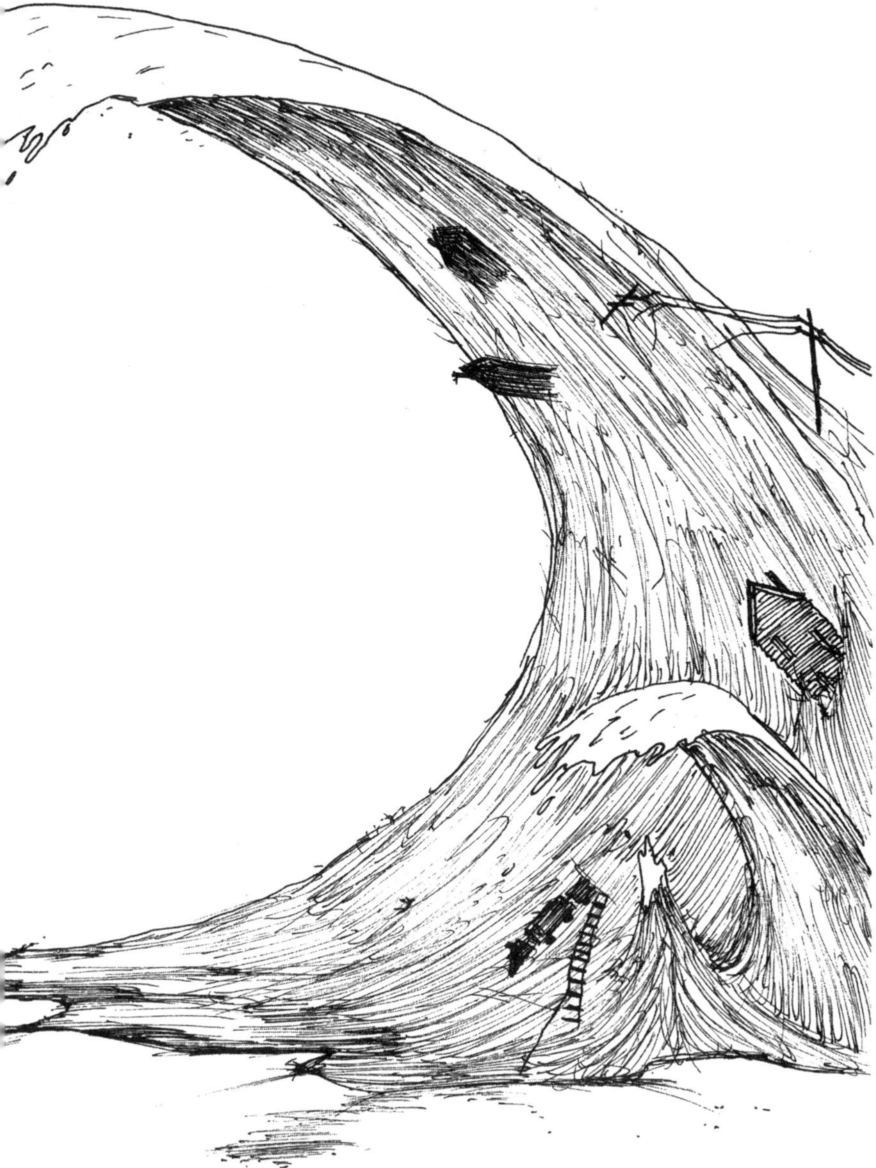

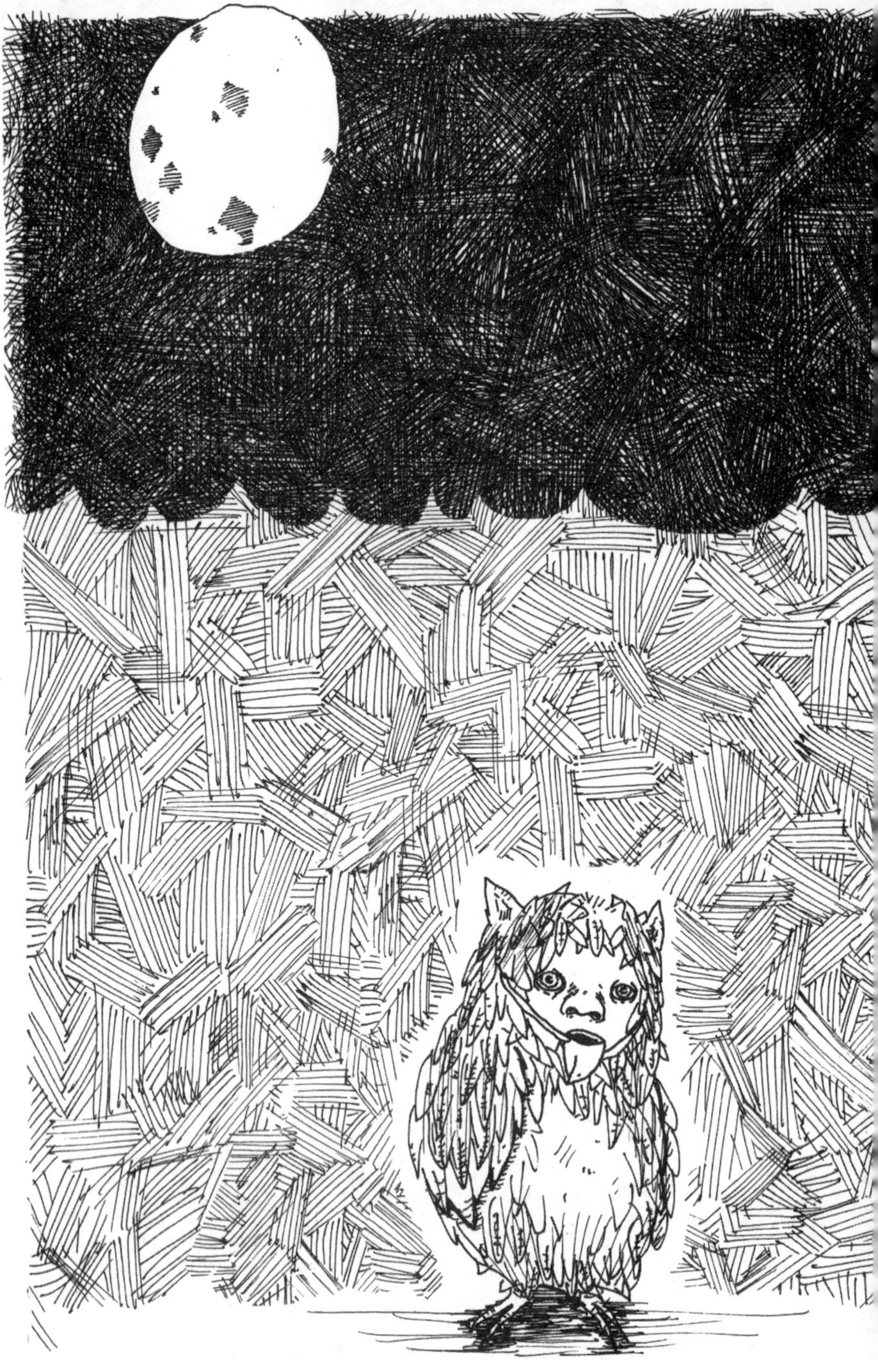

Waiting like a song to be sung,
Hidden in the cleft of the night.

Listen!

And when they went, I heard the sound of their wings like the sound of many waters, like the sound of the Almighty.
Ezekiel 1:24

Before this album was *The Cymbal Crashing Clouds*, I was calling it *The Animist*. (I called it this mostly to myself; no one else cares what I'm thinking of writing next.) The idea came to me one day when my brother remarked that my son Jude was "a little animist," talking to his trains and plastic men as if they had eternal souls. I overheard this and thought that I ought to write an album of songs ascribing souls—or at least voices—to inanimate, everyday things. I later abandoned the title because of its pagan implications. But *The Cymbal Crashing Clouds* is really just another way of getting at the same idea.

I knew that if I were to write such an album it would have to begin with a prelude similar to the one from William Blake's *Songs Of Innocence*. In it, like Blake, I would encounter the muse in some form and be commissioned to write the songs that followed.

I have always loved the prophetic visions of the Bible. Though I am not even a *minor* prophet (nor a prophet at all), "Listen!" is my imagined vision. It was the last song I wrote for the record, mainly because it was the most ambitious in concept and the most challenging to write. It also came last because I was waiting for the muse. Blake's appeared to him as a baby on a cloud. Mine took a different form. And he took his time.

The first stanza describes a street in Brunswick, Maryland, where I stood at four in the morning waiting for a ride to the airport after a week spent working on the *Carousel Rogues* record. The imagery here is borrowed from the fourth chapter of Revelation. The cars clothed in white blossoms represent the twenty-four elders. The row houses are the creatures covered with eyes. The box elder seeds falling are seraphim. The opening line alone is an exception, with its reference to Moses hidden in the cleft of the rock, waiting for his own vision of the Lord. Together, these images are clues that the silent street may be more than it seems, and that the silence here is pregnant with the anticipation of some imminent arrival.

I pass through a door in a dream,
Hidden in the cleft of the night
Among the parked cars lining the street,
Robed in petals of white,
Where the seeds spin down from the trees—
Whirling angels in free flight—
And the houses mutter in their sleep,
Covered in shuttered eyes.

In the second stanza, the description of the approaching train is drawn from the first chapter of Ezekiel, in which God appears to the prophet on a stormy wind and a dark cloud flashing with fire. There in the dark hills of the Northeast, the fire was burning in the throat of a great locomotive running down the rails on wheels within wheels. I hope comparing the train cars to "the tails of his coal-black coat" evokes both the train of God's robe filling the temple in the prophet Isaiah's vision and also the coat tails of a great conductor entering the orchestra pit. Working out these lines, I envisioned Bugs Bunny, disguised as the conductor Leopold Stokowski, gliding through the pit—the awed musicians turning all colors as his glove, floating in the air by itself, holds the final note out into infinity.

Shrouded in steam and smoke,
On a dark cloud he approaches;
And the tails of his coal-black coat
Are a train of lumbering coaches.
He passes unseen like a ghost,
But he thunders like a herd of horses.
And he calls to the heavenly host
To join with their airy voices.

I was unaware of the train as it drew near. Brunswick is a tiny railroad town, so all her residents are barely aware of the constant racket of the cars in the yard nearby. But as I stood in that street alone, bleary-eyed from lack of sleep, the train whistle blew. It couldn't have been more than half a mile away, so it was wonderfully loud. It was the most beautiful, mournful sound, and it not only saturated the air around me, but it filled me up as well. I felt that it overflowed my sense of hearing and then spilled over into all my other senses. When it ceased, still it echoed and echoed, and now it occurred to me that I was hearing not the train whistle itself, but all the world speaking it back to me—a wordless word repeated by the flat faces of buildings and billboards. All the angels of the atmosphere were singing it with their elemental voices.

I knew this was not the voice of the Lord, but I also knew that if I had ever heard the voice of the Lord I had heard it in the same way. *Long ago, at many times and in many ways, God spoke to our fathers by the prophets, but in these last days he has spoken to us by his son.* (Hebrews 1:1)

And that Word he has spoken pools in the hollows of the world and pours forth daily in all manner of ecstatic utterances. Before I wake, the Word arrives at my door in the sun's daily bulletin. In the afternoon he rends the veil of grey clouds. At dusk he bleeds red and dies.

I sleep. I rise.

Meanwhile, the eye is ever receiving, ever transmitting. In my ear, the hammer and the anvil tap out their constant missive. It reads, "A Name A Name A Name."

I owe the image of owl's wings brushing my eyes to the room full of ravens in a book called *Jonathan Strange and Mr. Norrell* by Susanna Clarke. If you've read the book, you'll recognize this as another prophetic vision of sorts.

The whistle blast echoes so loud
That it rings the bell of the sky—
A song that sounds and resounds;
An unbearable, aching sigh;
Like a parliament of owls—
Silver wings brushing my eyes;
Crossing arms drawing the phrase out,
Holding the moment in time.

Now, in this fourth stanza, the tone of the lyric changes to prayer and provocation. "If you're going to ring the bell of the sky, I say, then by all means strike up the band!" *Lord, not my feet only but also my hands and my head!* (John 13:9)

Andrew Peterson once told me the story of Nikola Tesla's "little black box," which could determine the resonant frequency of a building and then generate that frequency in ever-increasing intensity until the building was swaying and threatening to come apart. I'm afraid I am a little dull and slow to take notice of things (ask my friends); so my prayer here is for God to sound the note that shakes my building, to wave his arms a bit and get my attention.

So signal the cymbal crashing clouds,
Pluck all the steeples and spires,
Cue the rivers with the reeds in their mouths,
Conduct the electrical choirs,
Rattle every window in town,
Strum all the telephone wires,
Crossing arms drawing the phrase out...

The fifth stanza is not the first time I have brazenly stolen from a Rich Mullins essay called "Playing Second Fiddle." In it, Rich imagined the awful emptiness a violin must feel, the horror and loneliness of being shut in its case, the terrible tension of its nerves now and again raked painfully by the bow. And he observed that the poor instrument is deaf to the music made through its suffering. Here in the last lines of the song I invite God to make whatever music he created me for, and the violence of the action is not accidental. I am a little afraid of what God might do to produce whatever sound I was intended for. And what shall I say? *"Father, save me from this hour?" But for this purpose I have come to this hour.* (John 12:27)

'Cause my bones are all bells to be rung;
My nerves are attuned and tight.
So come knock the air from my lungs
Out over the cords in my windpipe.
My skin pulled taut like a drum,
I am bracing myself for the strike.
Waiting like a song to be sung,
Hidden in the cleft of the night.

Maybe worth mentioning (and maybe not) is that I did most of the really difficult writing on a trip to Sweden with Andrew, much of which was spent riding on trains. In fact, I appropriately recorded the first bits of the music (though not the train whistles themselves) on a passenger train. I might also mention that the title is a play on "Look!" which is a song from the lost Beach Boys album, *Smile*. In fact, a sort of marketing slogan for that record was "Look! Listen! Vibrate! Smile!" This is the first of many references (musical and lyrical) to *Smile* on *The Cymbal Crashing Clouds*.

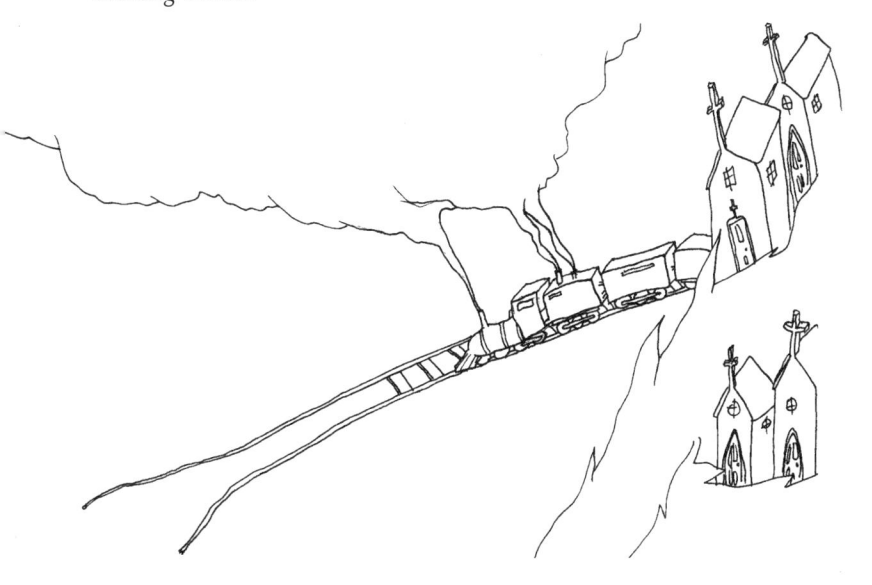

E G B D F

Part I: The Bust Of Beethoven

When I was a young piano student, it was widely known (because I had made it widely known) that I could play Beethoven's "Für Elise." It was a little advanced for me, but I could *just* pull it off. Other kids recognized the tune and it sounded even harder than it was, so it made for a good parlor trick. And it made me feel like I had potential.

But if it was up to me to pick what played in the tape deck of my mom's wood-paneled station wagon, it was a toss-up between Weird Al's *Even Worse* and The Beach Boys' *Endless Summer*. Beethoven wasn't even in the glove box. It had never occurred to me to listen to the music I practiced in my lessons; nor had I ever thought to learn the music I listened to in the car. And this disconnect didn't bother me.

But my failures as a piano student bothered me a great deal. "Für Elise" was about as far as I ever got. I rarely practiced, and my teacher knew it. I remember my eight-year-old self staring straight ahead at the music on the page, willing my fingers to obey, all the while aware of the disapproving gaze of the figure fixed atop Mrs. H's upright piano—the frowning bust of Beethoven, which, in the song, represents the law of Moses, staring down at us from on high, severe and unmoving, impossible to satisfy.

The work of the law is written on their hearts, while their conscience also bears witness, and their conflicting thoughts accuse or even excuse them.
Romans 2:15

Before we ever take a lesson, we know intuitively that good boys do fine. We don't need a piano teacher or a starch-collared preacher to teach us. But as a kid, I was *not* doing fine and I knew that just as well. I believed in God as a matter of fact, but I dabbled in sin as a matter of curiosity, and the law glowered at me as if to say, "You ought to be ashamed of yourself." So I was ashamed of myself. I hid from God in the garden. I covered my nakedness. I made lifeless idols of sin and self, and the disconnect between what I practiced and what I loved grew. But I learned to live with it, as we all do, and tried not to look the law in the eye.

And He said, "Go, and say to this people:

'Keep on hearing, but do not understand:
    keep on seeing but do not perceive.'
Make the heart of this people dull,
    and their ears heavy,
    and blind their eyes:
lest they see with their eyes,
    and hear with their ears,
and understand with their hearts,
    and turn and be healed."
Isaiah 6:9-10

But their minds were hardened. For to this day,
when they read the old covenant, that same veil remains unlifted.
2 Corinthians 3:14

Part II: Paul McCartney In Day-Glo
The lyric lies at this point: I never really played Nintendo when I should have been practicing—I watched my

older brother play! He would have given me my turn, but I was happier just observing. I wasn't very good after all, and I didn't really enjoy dying over and over.

We liked to mute the game so we could listen to records. *Sgt. Pepper's Lonely Hearts Club Band* was the jewel of my dad's collection. So while Josh played Zelda, I would listen to "A Day in the Life" and stare at that famous photo inside the jacket: the Beatles dressed in day-glo, smiling against a canary yellow background. Then it was the Red and Blue Beatles collections, and then Paul Simon's *Graceland*, and then *A Liturgy, A Legacy, and A Ragamuffin Band*, and so on.

Meanwhile, I was on the decline as a piano student. My first piano teacher had fired me. I had a new teacher, but I still dreaded lessons. To me, piano was all about beating a piece of music and then trying to beat a harder piece of music. It was basically a video game. And I didn't really enjoy dying over and over. Eventually, I gave it up.

But all the while I was falling deeper in love with records, and it was only a year or two before those records brought me right back to the piano. This time, however, I wasn't trying to beat any bosses—I was learning to speak a language. I started transcribing solos from jazz albums and reading books about music theory. I taped sheets of paper with chord voicings written on them all around the house to help me memorize them. I was practicing scales with a metronome. I was working out tough passages at slow tempos, speeding them up incrementally until I could play them at full speed. Love had motivated in me a more rigorous discipline than my teachers could have ever asked for. It was a new beginning. Beethoven had killed me utterly, but Paul McCartney revived me. *For to set the mind on the flesh is death, but to set the mind on the Spirit is life and peace.* (Romans 8:6)

*"But this is the covenant that I will make with
the house of Israel after those days, declares the LORD:
I will put my law within them, and I will write it on their hearts.
And I will be their God, and they shall be my people."*
Jeremiah 31:33

*"And it shall come to pass afterward,
 that I will pour out my Spirit on all flesh:
your sons and your daughters shall prophesy,
 your old men shall dream dreams,
 and your young men shall see visions."*
Joel 2:28

*And we all, with unveiled face, beholding the glory of the Lord,
are being transformed into the same image
from one degree of glory to another.*
2 Corinthians 3:18

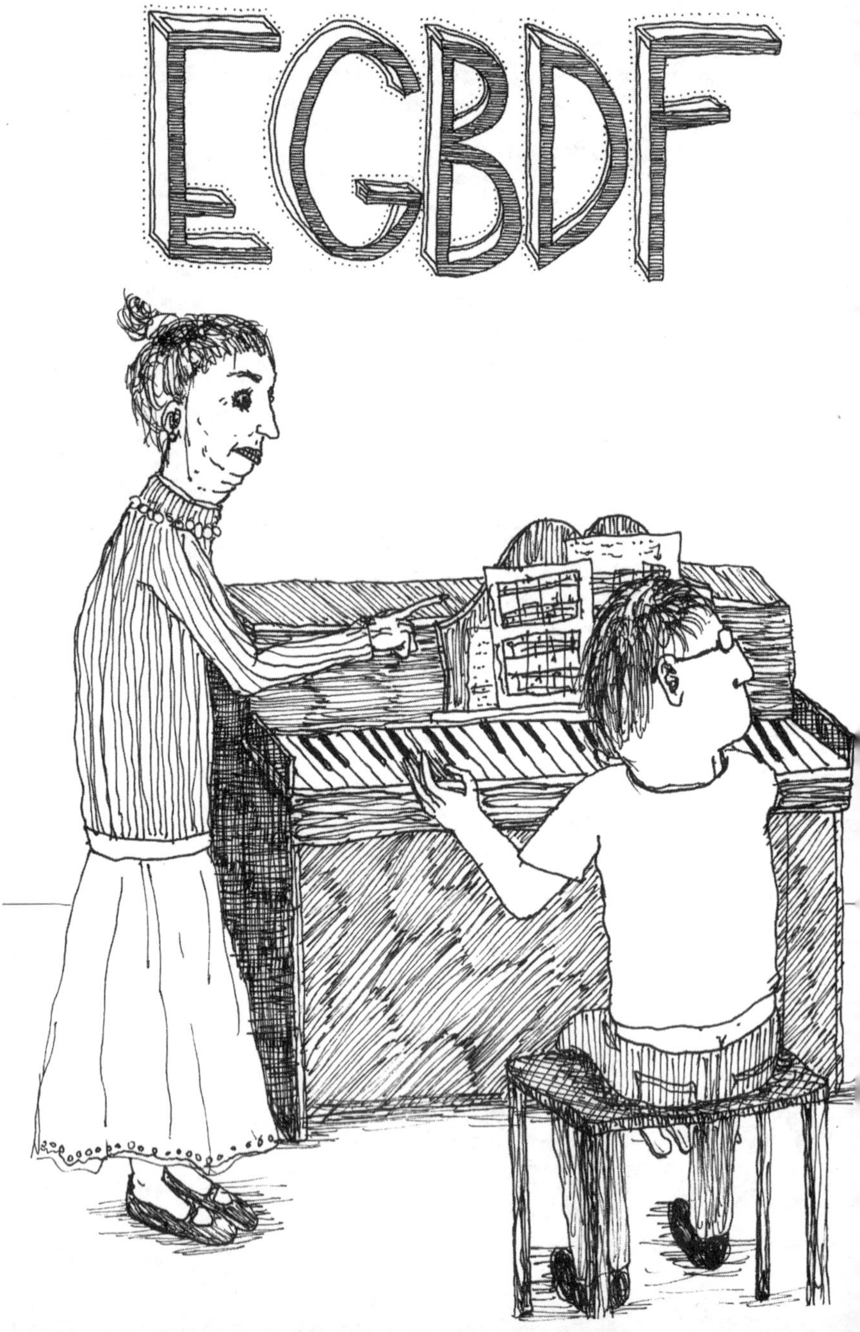
EGBDF

I was staring at the stern
   facial features of
Ludwig Von Beethoven,
And my prim piano teacher in her seventies
Thought I wasn't listening.
But despite my ADD, what she said to me
I remember perfectly:

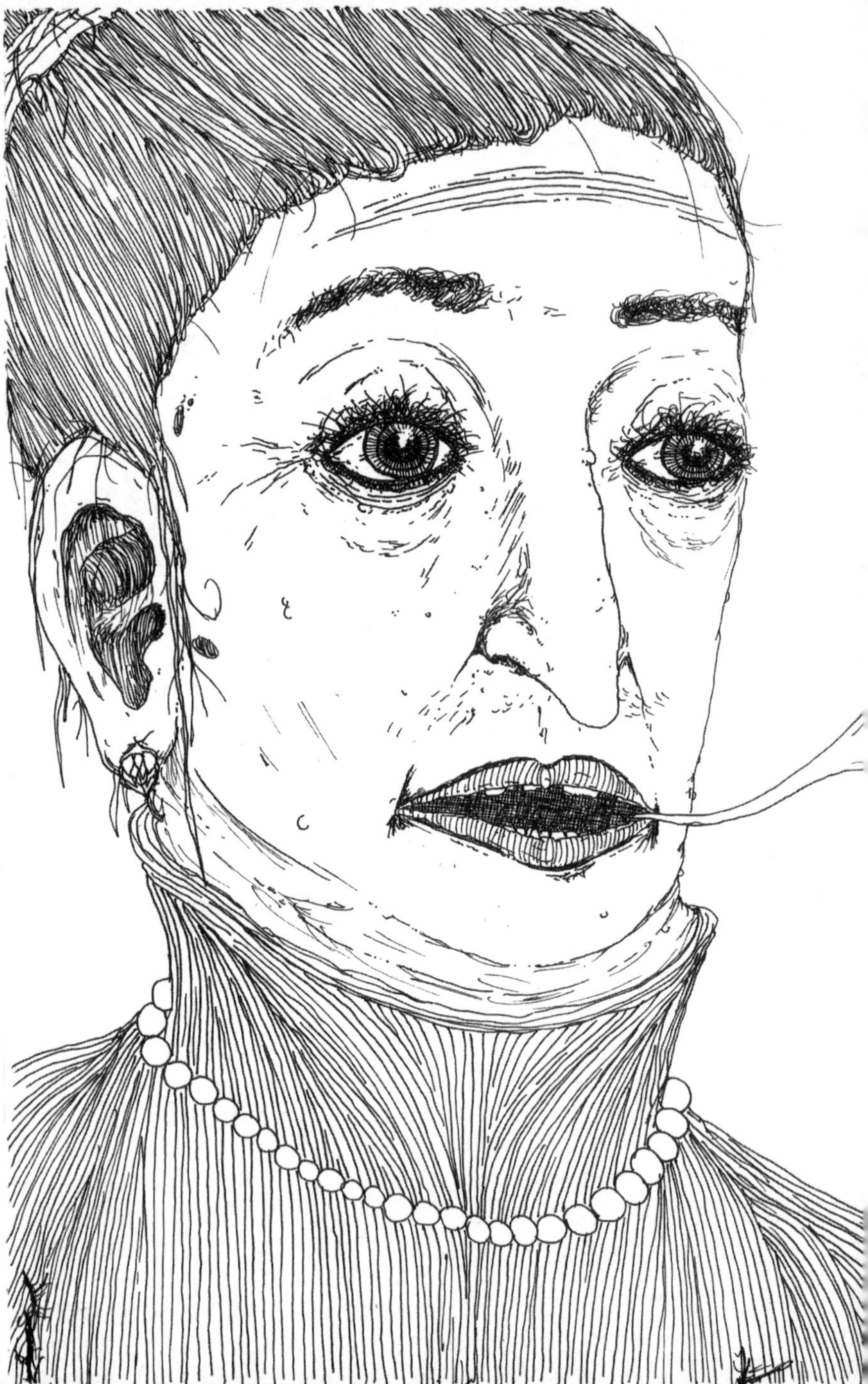

Every
Good
Boy
Does
Fine

There were venerated volumes of rhythm
   and melody—
The grave embalmings of a language
   dead for a century;
To read, to recite, to repeat,
Without even thinking to learn to speak

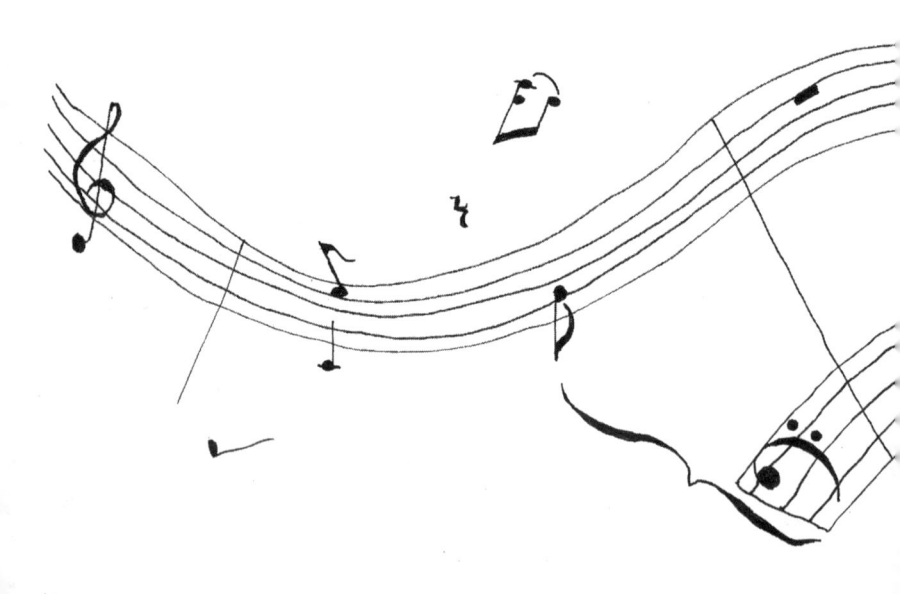

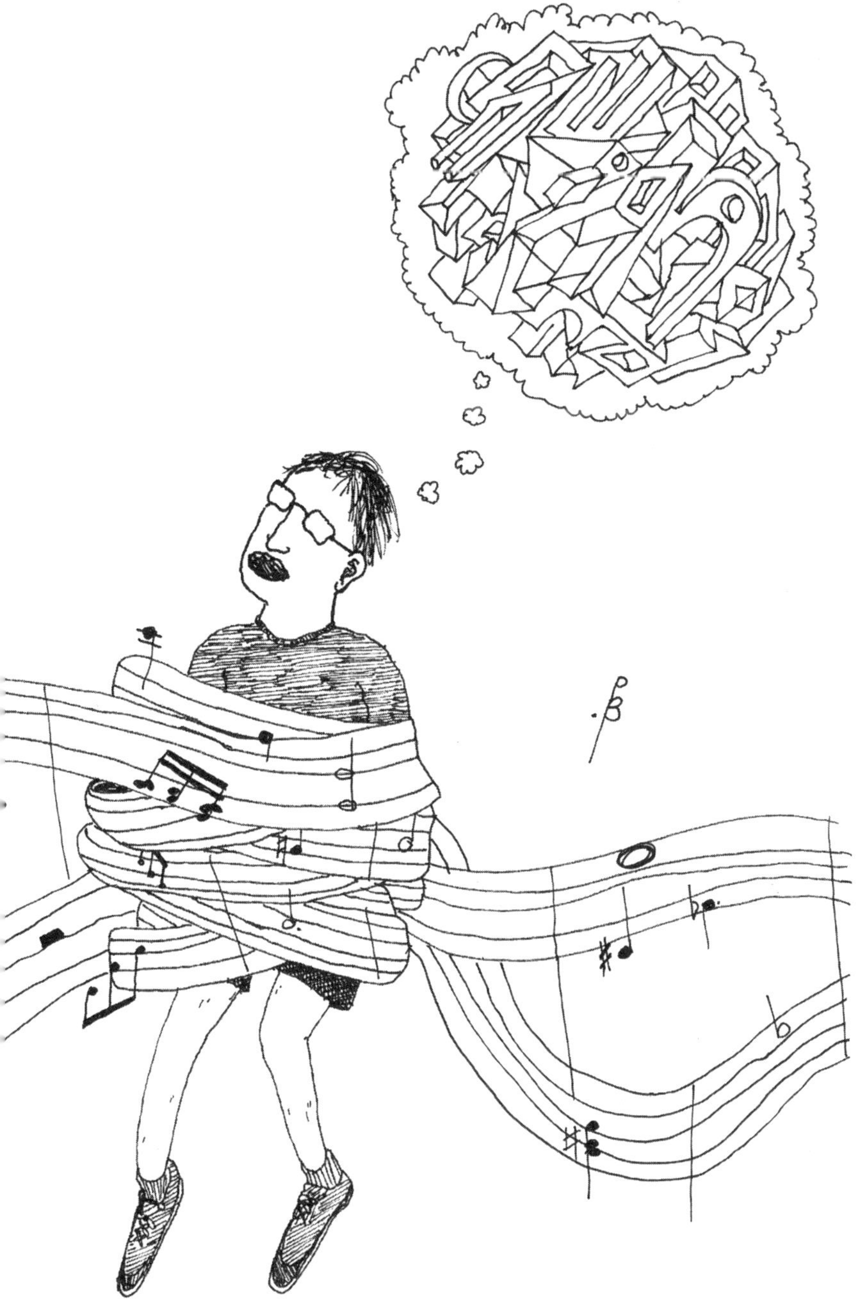

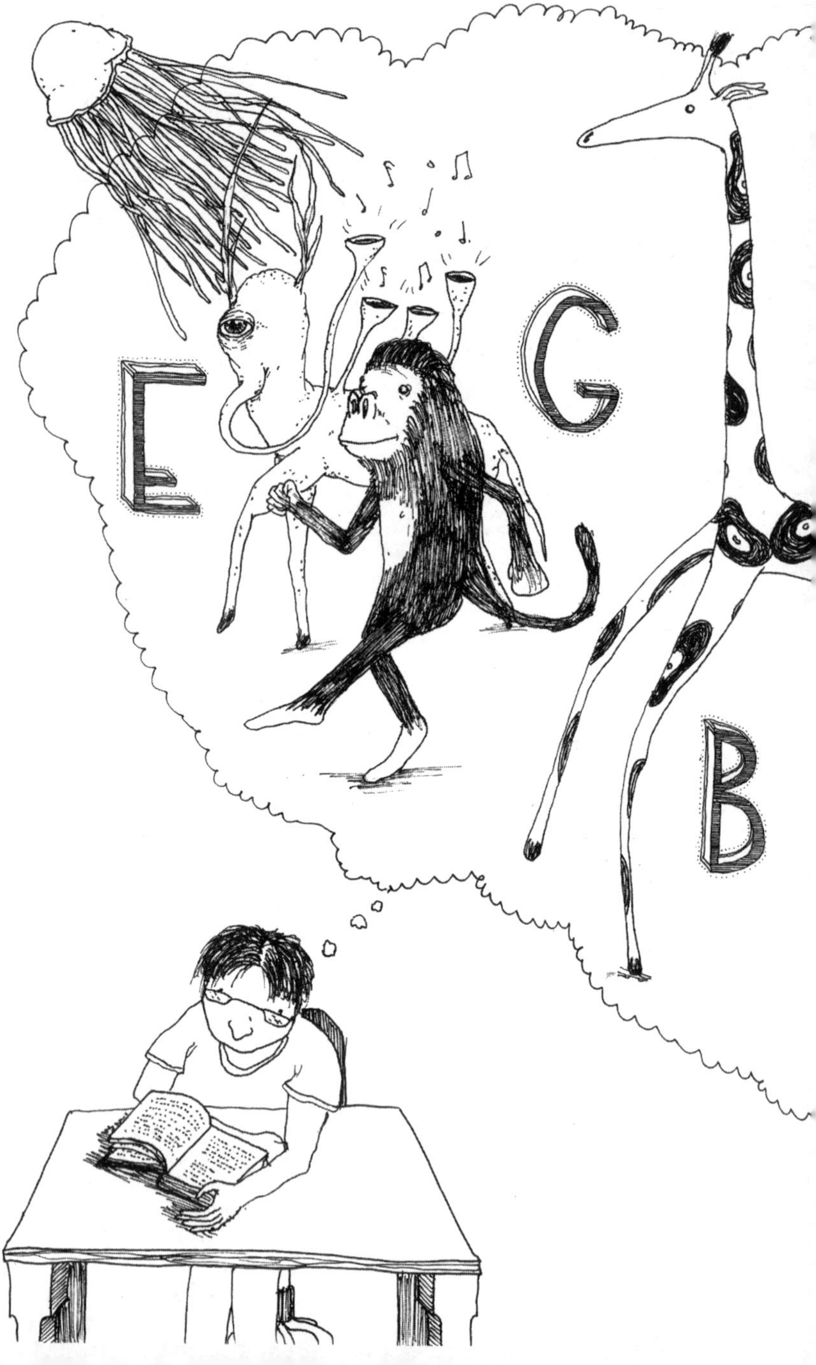
E
G
B

'Cause good boys do fine
Always hearing,
We never understand.
We see without perceiving
And speak of what we can't comprehend.

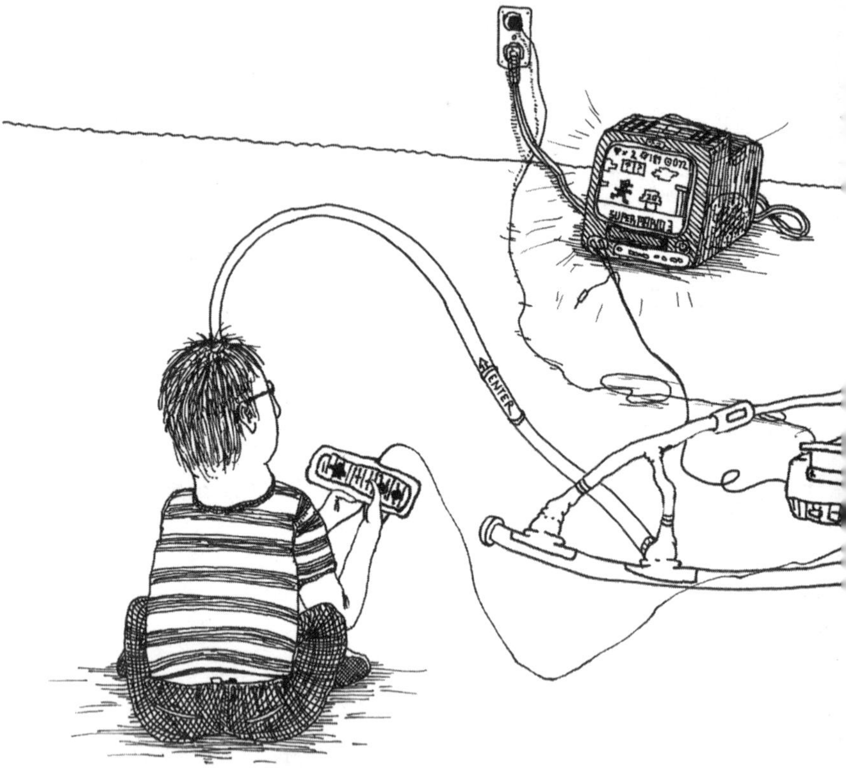
ENTER

Well, Mrs. H was unimpressed,
Though I had practiced religiously.
Never mind that I was practicing
To master Super Mario 3.
And soon she put my memory behind her
And fired me with the biting reminder
That every good boy does fine.

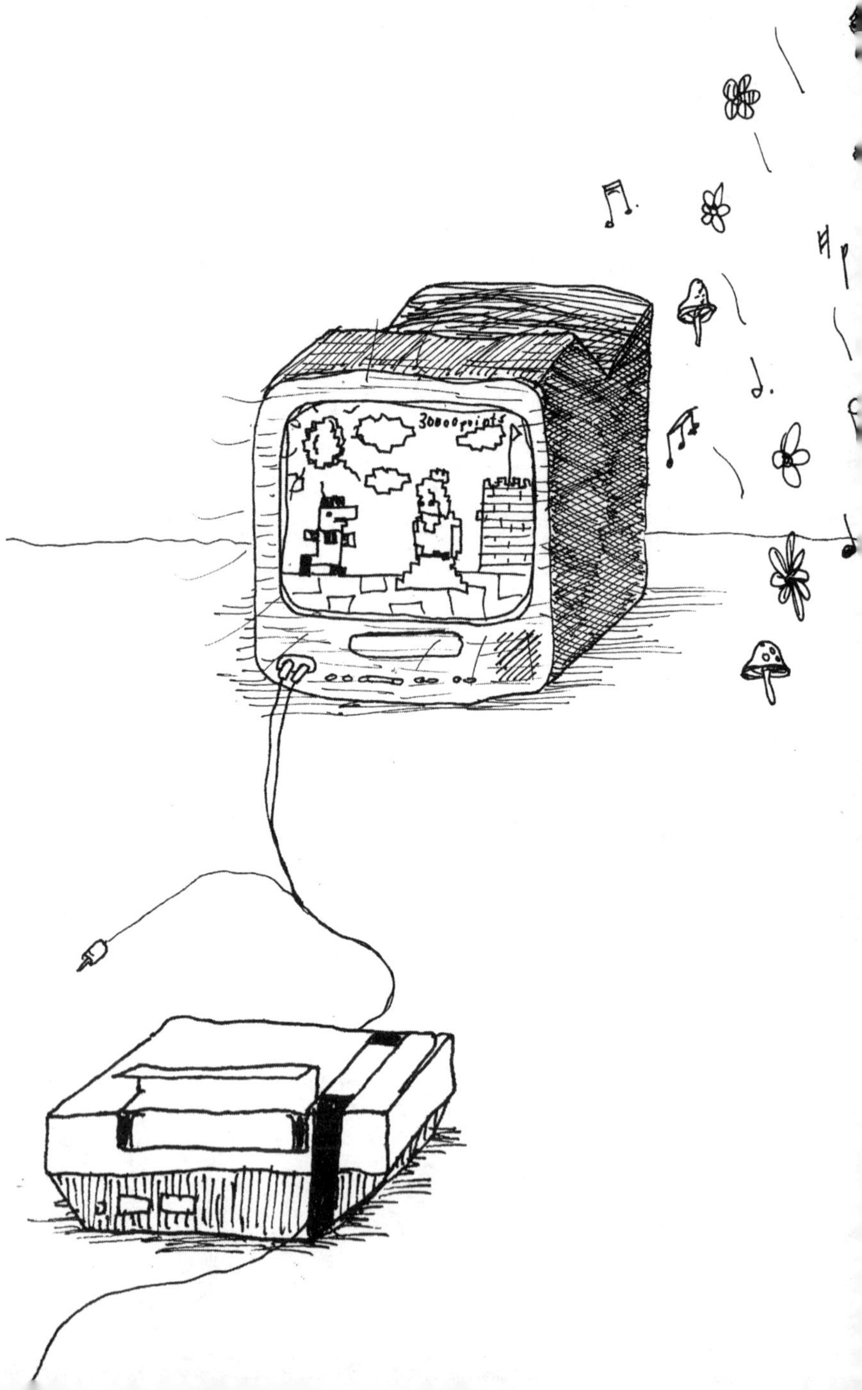
30000points

So I was left to pursue my own endeavors:
Saving pixelated princesses
While listening to records.
So it was Shigeru Miyamoto
Who first introduced me to Sergeant Pepper
And his Lonely Hearts Club Band.

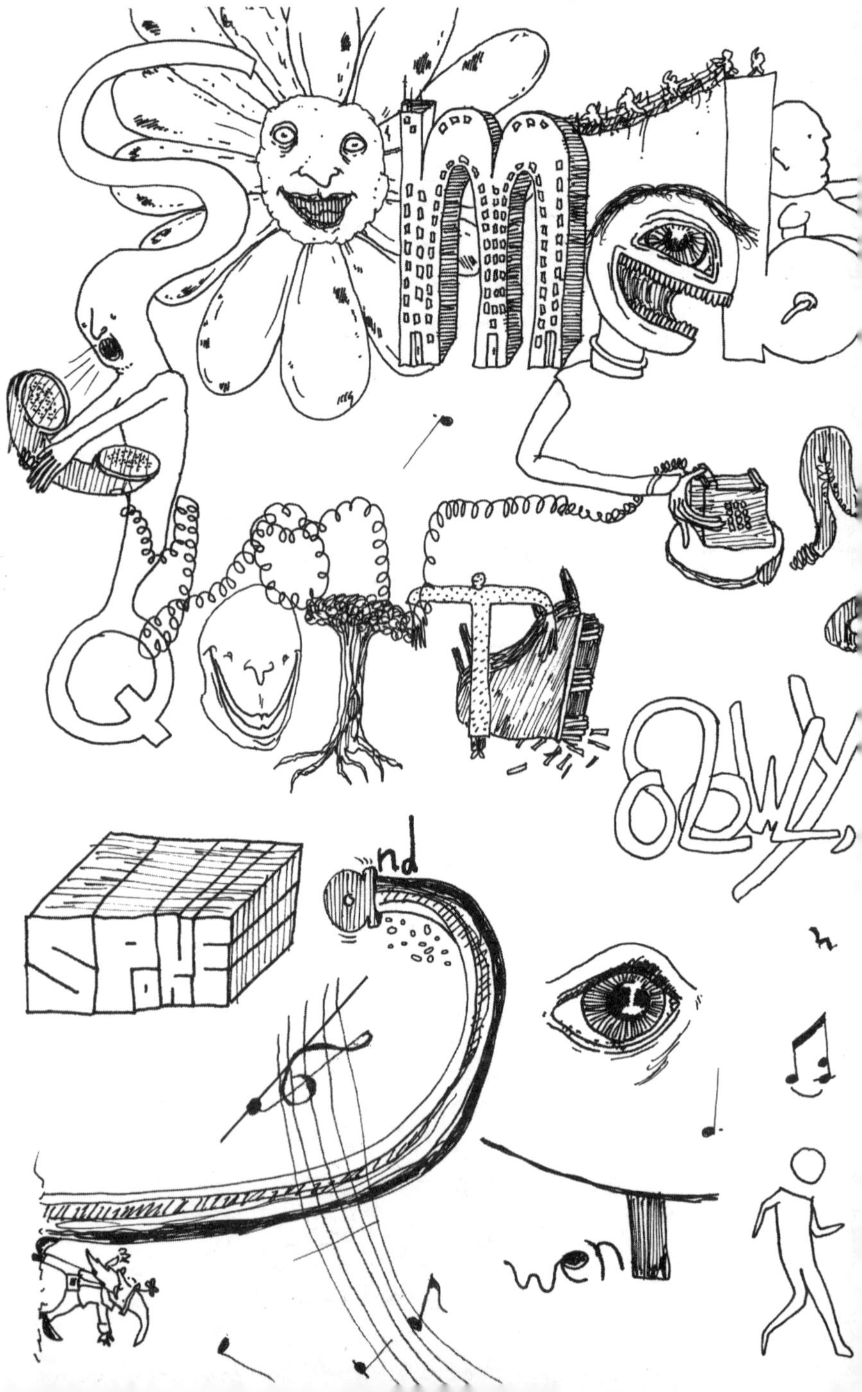

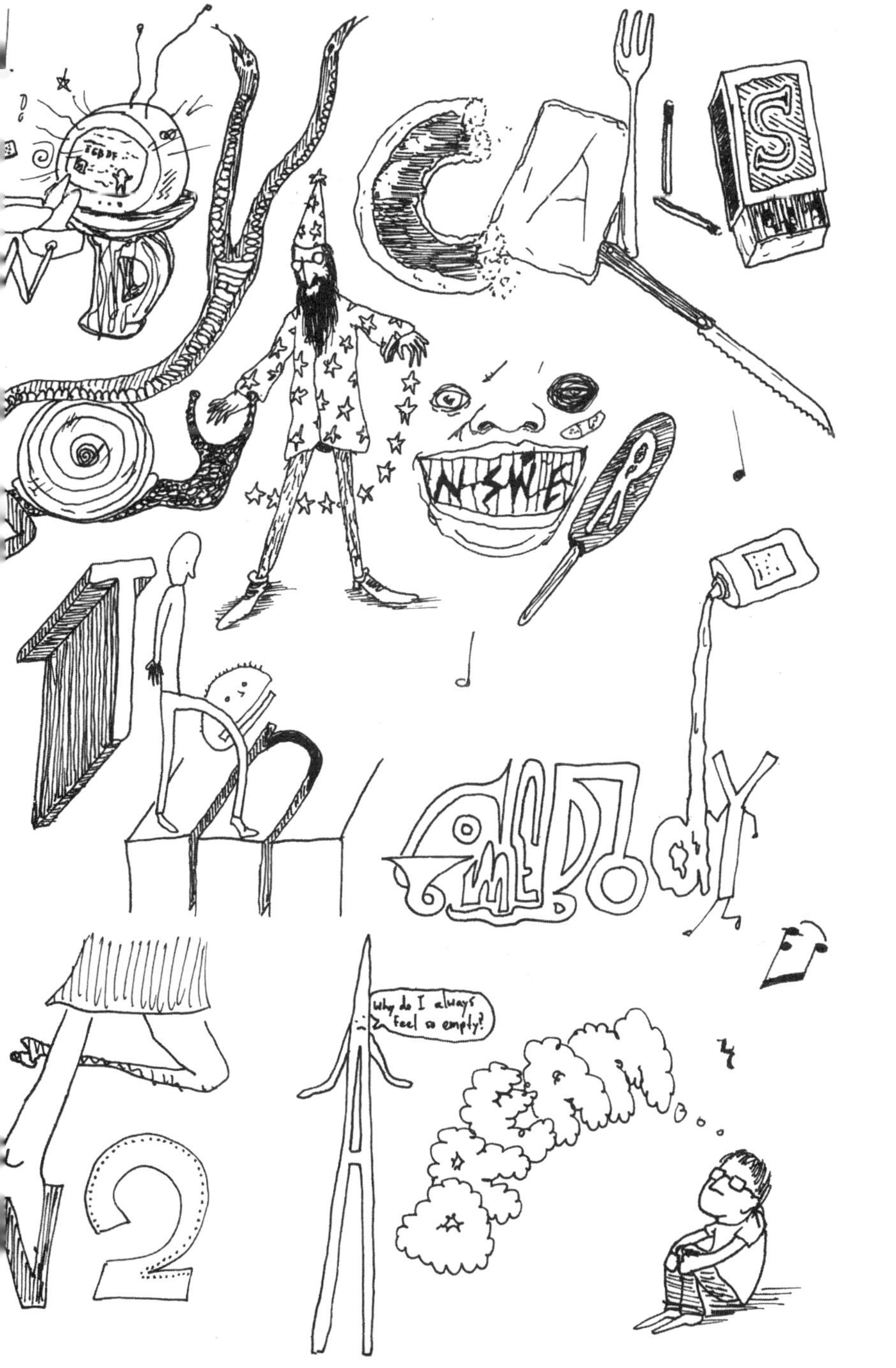
why do I always feel so empty?

Sir Paul McCartney appeared to me in Day-Glo
With an english horn,
Speaking words I thought were dead,
Now strangely reborn.
And I heard unearthly voices
That sang in distant doorways and rooms.
He was conducting kite strings,
Winds that filled me and I flew.
And when I came to…

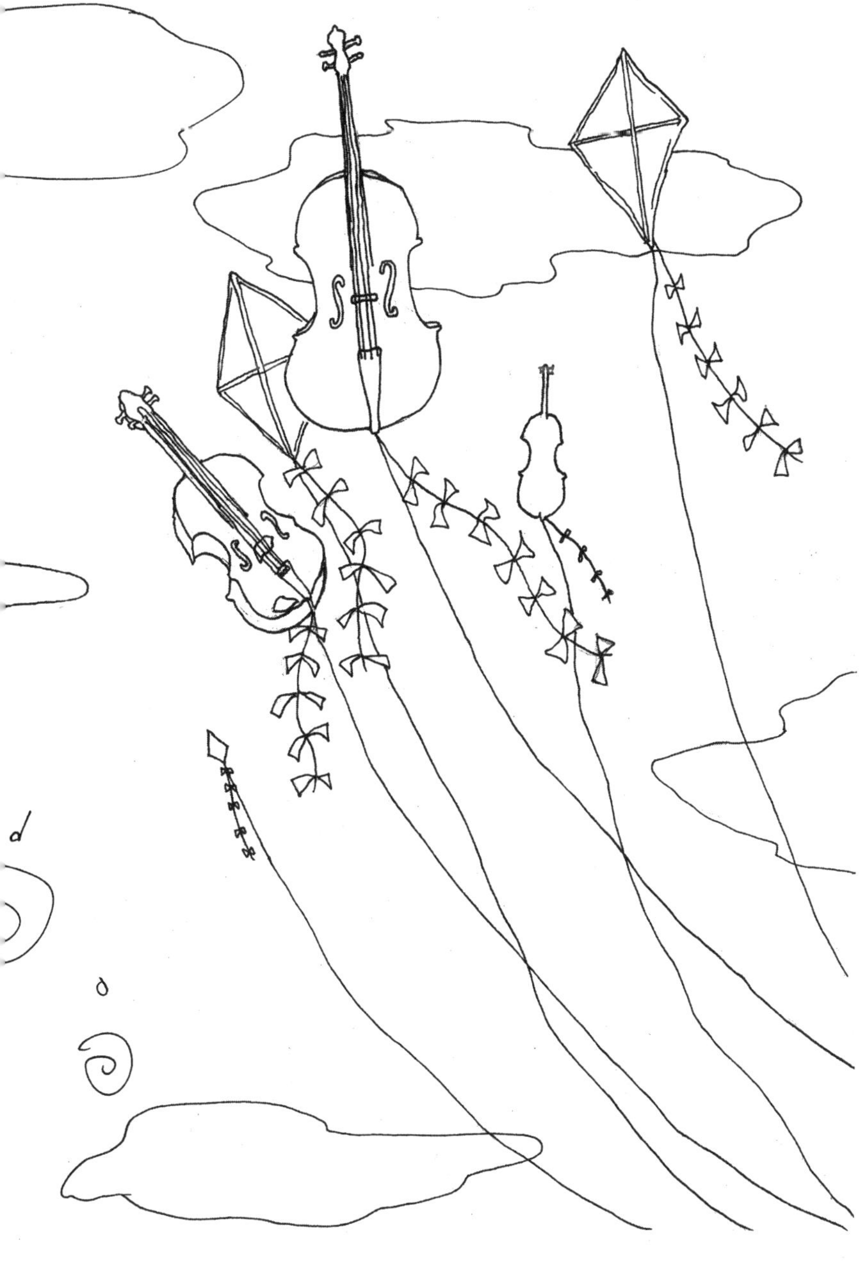

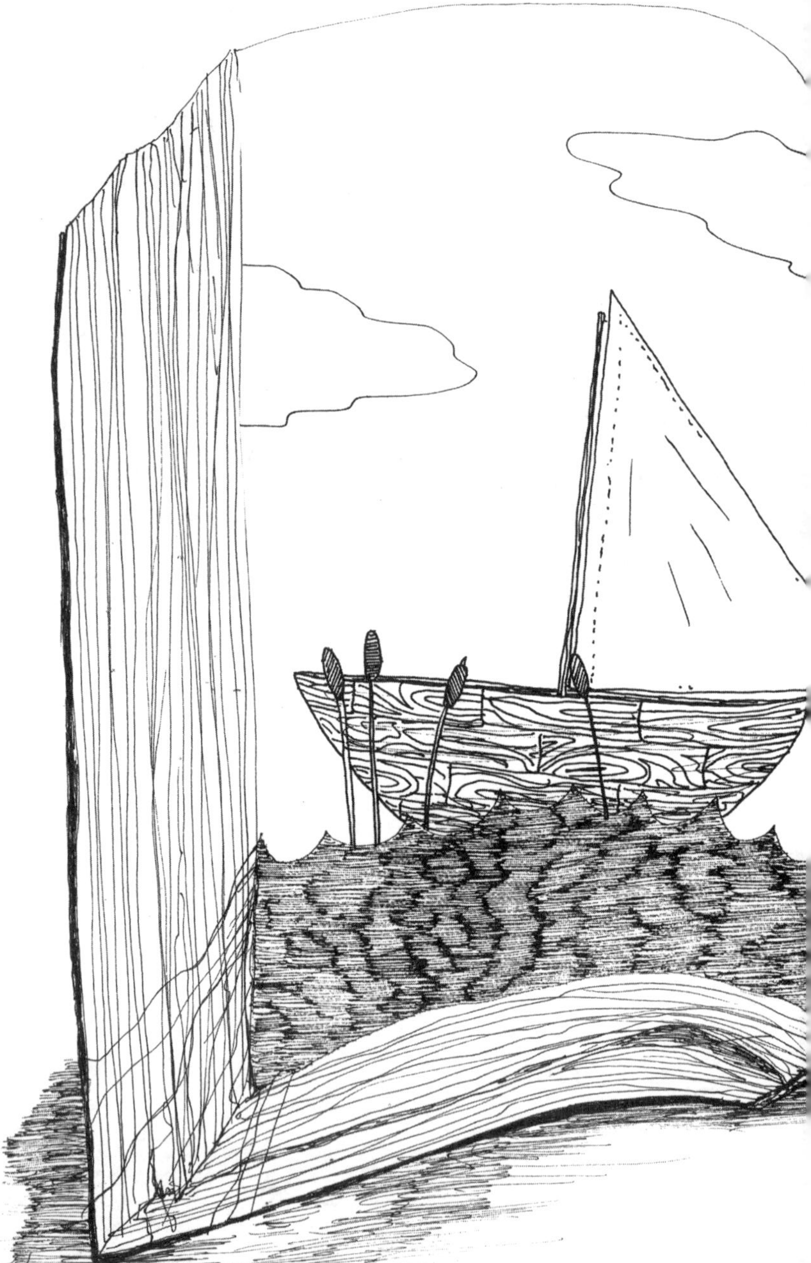

I was trying to find with pen and ink
The passages to pass between our souls,
Panning ordinary rivers on rumors of gold.

And beside me in the coffee shops,
They're lost in dreams and visions,
And they're filling Moleskine notebooks
With their compositions
Like it's a competition.
(I guess it is?)

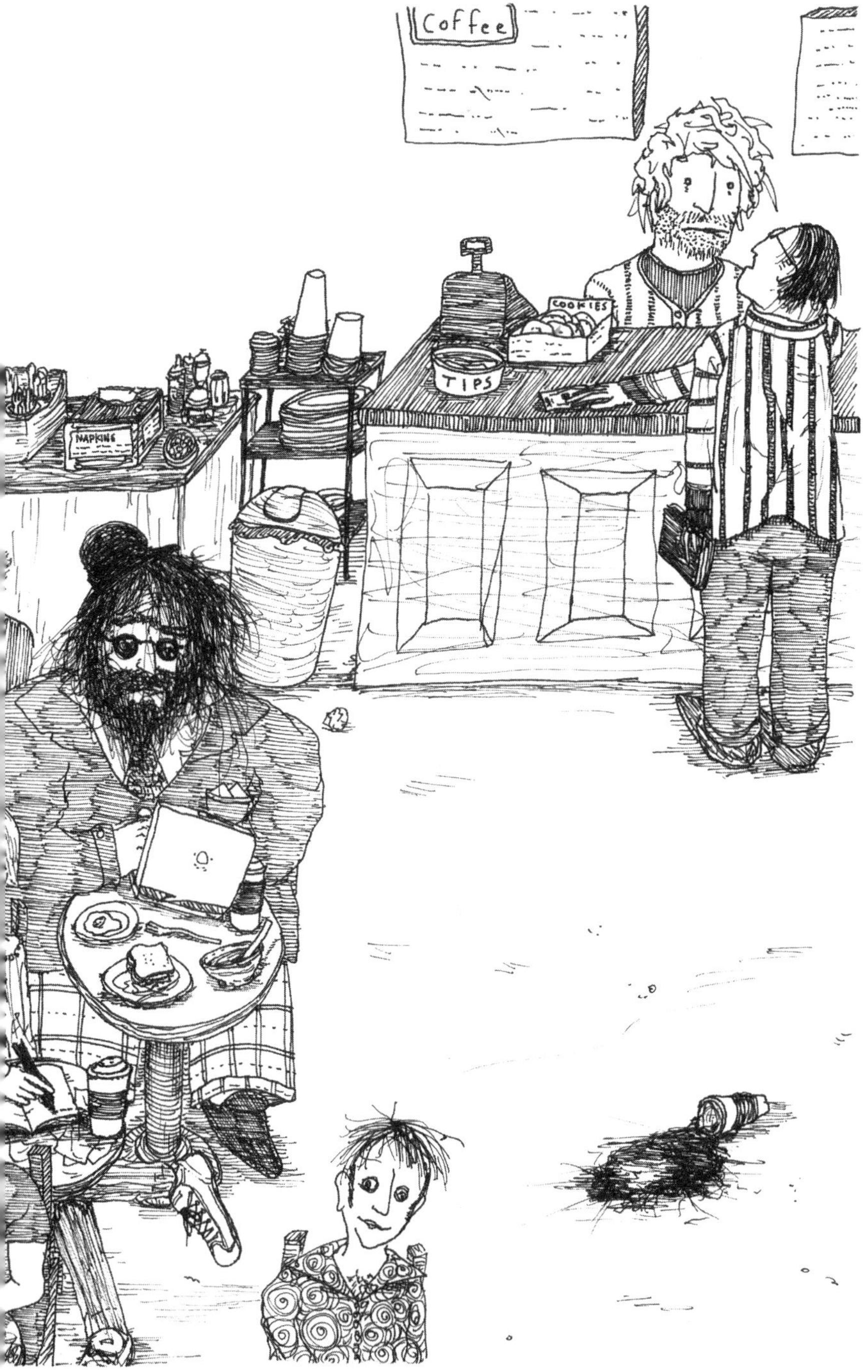
Coffee
COOKIES
TIPS
NAPKINS

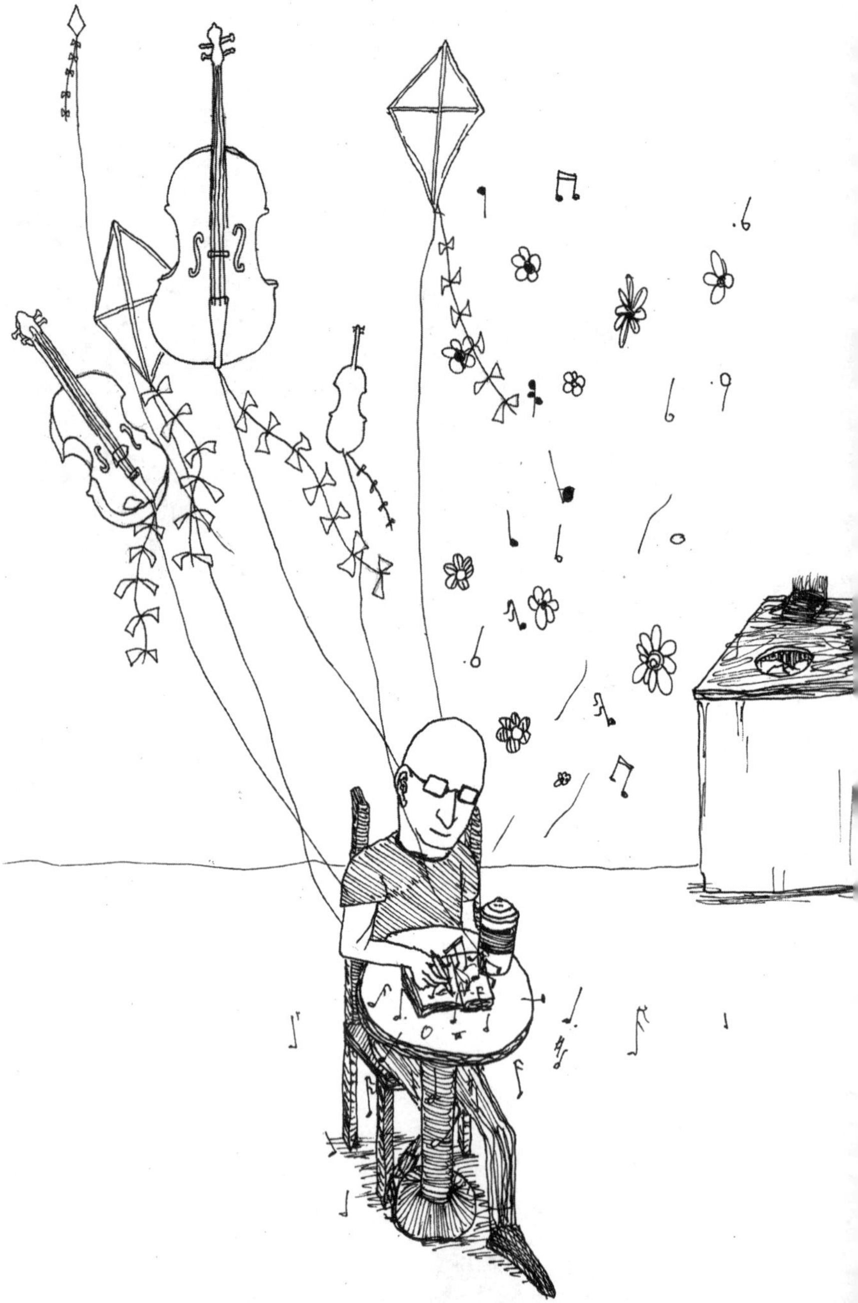

Now the harmony is written on my heart;
Yeah, the language is on my tongue.
And I barely understand it,
But I've only just begun.

EVERY GOOD BOY DOES

Fine

Sorry But I'm Yours

Sometimes I get a little nervous;
Sometimes I get the shakes.
If I can't pull myself together
They're gonna boo me off stage.

I know you don't ask much of me,
But I'm gonna fail you, I'm afraid,
And all that I can say is

I'm sorry,
But I'm yours.

Who slipped the keys of the cherry-red Camaro
In the pocket of the town drunk?
And what do you get when you send your only
  daughter
To the prom with a young punk?

I warned you, but you wouldn't leave me be.
And now, after all you've seen,
If you still believe in me, I'm sorry.

Say I'm getting better all the time.
But if that's a lie,
Oh well, never mind—
Just say you love me.

When I want to do right, evil lies close at hand.
Romans 7:21

My poor, timid voice wants only to live a quiet life, tending little gardens of conversation. But instead he is made something of a sideshow, rudely shoved in front of microphones and made to sing my songs.

But imagine *my* frustration. I work hard writing these things. Often they take years. Then I open my mouth and I'm something like the inverse of the singing frog in the cartoon. You see a man, but all you hear is "croak, croak."

I thought it was time we got some counseling. And I decided he should go first. So I wrote him a song of apology to sing to me from stage, and it has been surprisingly therapeutic for both of us.

The phrase "I'm sorry, but I'm yours" could be taken to mean "I know I'm a hopeless case, but at least I'm loyal," or it could mean "I hate to break it to you, but the fact is that you are stuck with me." Whichever you prefer.

Someone Is Asking

The city is a mirrorball,
Throwing rainbows around.
I listen to the whistle of the crosswalk cop,
Conducting the rhythm downtown;
And out the window of a passing car
Wedding bubbles are blowing in clouds.

I wonder what could it mean?

Could it mean that
Someone is asking to dance with me?

'Cause I see angels
Like a Reverend Finster painting
Hanging glowing garlands
From the rooftops of these rundown buildings,
Spilling gold and gilding all the sidewalks—

Reflecting the sky
To remind me
Someone is asking to dance with me,
Striking up the sappy saxophones and strings
Till all the angels of the atmosphere sing,
"Come and dance with me."

From steeple to steeple I am stringing thread.
From my window to your window I am leaving crumbs
  of bread.
From a star to a star to a star to a star...
Every movement has a meaning in this dance of ours.

The city is a royal ball,
Where we meet, where we fall...

Driving around Nashville, I had seen bubbles floating unaccountably through the air more than once in the span of a week. I knew there was no real explanation for this phenomenon. So it was my duty to make one up.

God, I decided, must be asking me to dance. And now that I thought of it, I saw coaches and footmen everywhere.

He makes his messengers winds, his ministers a flaming fire.
Psalm 104:4

You just have to keep your eyes peeled to see them.

The last bit of the lyric is inspired by a quotation from Arthur Rimbaud that I read in Annie Dillard's *Pilgrim at Tinker Creek*:

I have stretched ropes from steeple to steeple: garlands from window to window; golden chains from star to star; and I dance.

If my senses are tethered to my brain like kites on strings, and if my brain is tied to itself by a web of neurons ever signaling one another in the dark, it is so that I might make correlation after correlation—until the book of Scripture and the book of nature are married in my mind, until all the pins on the map are connected with yarn, like Jacob's ladder wound around my fingers, the angels ascending and descending.

The Fall

The leaf that budded green and grew
In the springtime, when the world was new,
Is growing old and changing now
From green to gold.

And all the shoes that shuffle through town
Drum a lullaby to lay the autumn down.
It's a tune that falls, diminishing,
And then resolves.

So this is the way the year ends:
Not with a bang, with a sigh.
Goodbye, old friend, goodbye.

The summer sun, once young and wild,
Is a little wiser and his eyes are tired;
He nods his head mid-afternoon
And then he's off to bed.

So while the days are ripe and sweet
We heap them up in baskets at our feet
And do our best to use them well,
'Cause they won't last.

Now the earth is prepared for her burial
Under snow upon snow.
And we wait and we wait for a miracle,
For the green fields to grow.

And this is the way the year ends:
With a sigh.
Goodbye, old friend,

Goodbye, goodbye, goodbye.

The leaf that budded green and grew
In the springtime, when the world was new,
Lets go at last
And settles in the withered grass.

I grew up listening to my dad's Vince Guaraldi records, especially a bright blue one called O Good Grief. Guaraldi had this pet chord progression

and he used it over and over. You could say he was a one-trick pony. Or you could say this was Charlie Brown's leitmotif. Doesn't matter. If your heart's in good working order that little set of changes will get you every time.

My favorite song on that album is called "Great Pumpkin Waltz." It sounds like a town square where leaves rustle as cartoon characters make their way home from school. I wrote the lines from "The Fall" about the shuffling shoes drumming a lullaby that diminishes and resolves as an ode to the Great Pumpkin and to Mr. Guaraldi's favorite progression.

How can you still write about the seasons? What new metaphor could you possibly employ? But then how can you not write about that set of changes that gives form to the melody of our days, that draws the phrase out over dissonances toward some hopeful resolution?

The summer was fecund. Life swarmed so thick around us we shooed it away. The sun burned with an unending heat. But then it ended after all.

Winter is the stark tonic, the note of finality. She covers the earth in a blanket of snow and turns out the light. And then there is the long sleep.

And then the sudden joyous turn.

Fall, however, is a softly whispered word in the warm embrace of a girl, her face a flush of color. Fall is that perfect penultimate change. She lays the days down in the leaves. "Hush," she says.

Who composed this progression of life, death, and resurrection? He played the head* with his right hand, comp'ed the chords with his left. And now my life and yours are lines he improvises over the same set of changes.

*"Head" refers to the melody of a jazz composition, which is generally played before the musicians improvise solos over the same chords. "Comp'ed" is short for "accompanied" and refers to the way a jazz rhythm section plays chords to back up the soloist.

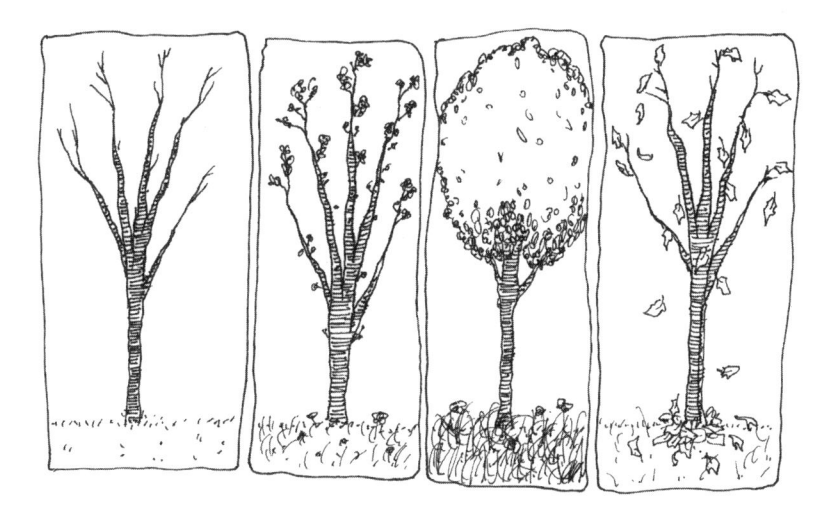

Shooting The Moon

Okay,
Deal me in,
But I can never fake it;
When I've got a pair of aces,
It's written on my face.

I just think I know
A good hand
When I hold it,
And I don't walk away—
I'll stay.

It used to be
If my eyes were open
I was looking out
for number one.
It was a lonely life.

So if it's gonna be you and me,
It's each for the other, baby,
From now on.

'Cause all my eggs are in one basket;
All my money's on you.

I know it's a gamble,

But if all that I'm holding's
A two of a kind
I'll be betting on you

With my last dime.
And maybe I might be
out of my mind,
But you know I'll stay.

I'll never leave you.

I know it's a gamble,
But I'm shooting the moon.

The risky thing about trying to really love your wife is that once you've defected to her side who will be left to man your battle stations? If you don't go on the defensive, who will defend you? It's a suicide mission, no doubt. But you're going to die anyway. You might as well die for someone else.

She's Invincible

She's the kind of girl you can never get to;
Attracted to her,
But you can't break through.

She's invincible to me.

And she's supersonic;
Yeah, she find me just in time.
She pull me from the flame,
Yeah, she save me from the fire.

Then it's,
"Up, up, and away!"
And I'm feeling like a fool,
'Cause I'm the kind of loser
Who can never keep cool.

She's invincible to me,
And I'm invisible to her.

But how could she know
All the pain she's caused,
Tearing at my soul
With oblivious claws?

She's got a steel ribcage
And a bulletproof heart.

When my son Jude was three or four, he was a rock drummer. Now he's a promising pianist, the very image of composure and sophistication. But back in those savage days we had a sort of neo-punk band together in the shed. We had worked up some strong covers. Mostly it was the three B's: the Beatles, the Beach Boys, and Barney. This was all very smashing, but I felt we needed an original. So I came up with a guitar riff to the beat that Jude was best at and set to work on a lyric about a guy who's hopelessly in love with a girl who doesn't know he exists. By the time I finished it the band had broken up. We still eat breakfast together every day. Sometimes it's a little awkward.

I never expected this song to mean anything to anybody, but I guess it may come in handy for certain human males in moments of dire frustration.

The Fire Pit

When my little girl fell in
To the fire pit and the skin was ash
On her legs and back,

At first I cursed the thing:
Let it lie there, I said, smoldering.
Boarded up and aborted,
Damned and abandoned,
And left to die forever
For all I care.

But in the waiting room with shaky hands,
Long before the awful panic passed,
I softened.

And I swore we'd put this all behind us,
And one day the fire pit would remind us
Not of this night only,
But of others after;
Of the innocent light
And the dancing laughter
Of little girls chasing fireflies—
So close the open flame;
So perfectly unafraid.

"The Fire Pit" is based on a story that was told to me by my friend Josh Wright. Josh is a financial planner and a poet. I asked him to write his story down so that others could hear it as he told it to me—and so that someday, when he is Financial Poet Laureate, I can say I published him when.

"I spent the summer of 2009 laboring in my backyard to create an outside living area with an open fireplace. My family was anxious to put it to use, so in the early fall we christened the completed project with a get-together to watch a parade that would be passing through our neighborhood. We hoped earnestly for weather cool enough to welcome a fire and were excited when that was what we got. The party was a success, and after the crowd dispersed I set about cleaning up, still beaming with pride. My seven-year-old daughter worked alongside me, quickened by the prospect of going to Grandma's house when our job was done. She scurried back and forth around the fire pit, which held the glowing remnants of the morning's fire—until an innocuous little misstep sent her tottering toward the edge of the pit, where she fell and rolled, pressing her back and legs into the burning bed of coals."

"That afternoon in the emergency room, still unsure of what lay before us, I sat there unspeaking, full of guilt, regretting my summer's work. Some old part of me wanted to decommission the pit, to seal off the possibility of any future harm. But my wife comforted our little girl with promises that sometime soon this would all be over—that we'd be together at home, sitting around that same fire, roasting marshmallows, at ease and without pain. Deep within my wife lived the conviction that hurt will not just fade until it is forgotten but will be defeated so thoroughly that it will be made to serve us."

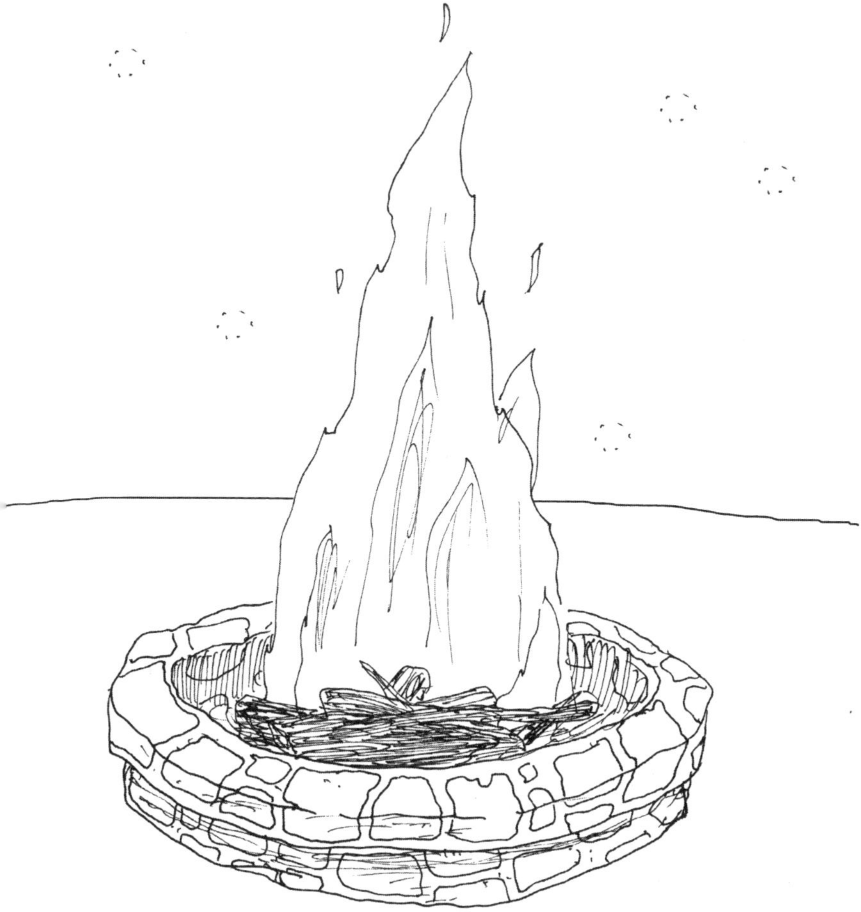

Your Secret Smile

What happens to
A dream that won't come true?
What have they done to you?

The doubting voice inside,
the poison in your mind,
They drain the light from your eyes
And they've stolen your soul.

So you hide
Your secret smile.

Summer's over soon;
They sold the old deuce coupe
And Brian's in his room

Wasted on cocaine
While jumbled reels of tape
Brilliantly pine away.

And now God only knows
Where you hide your smile.

Pray for an angel with an able ear—
A conscientious engineer—
To find the thread of melody
And mend your injured symphony.
Your voice will tremble as you sing—
A child again, remembering
Your smile.

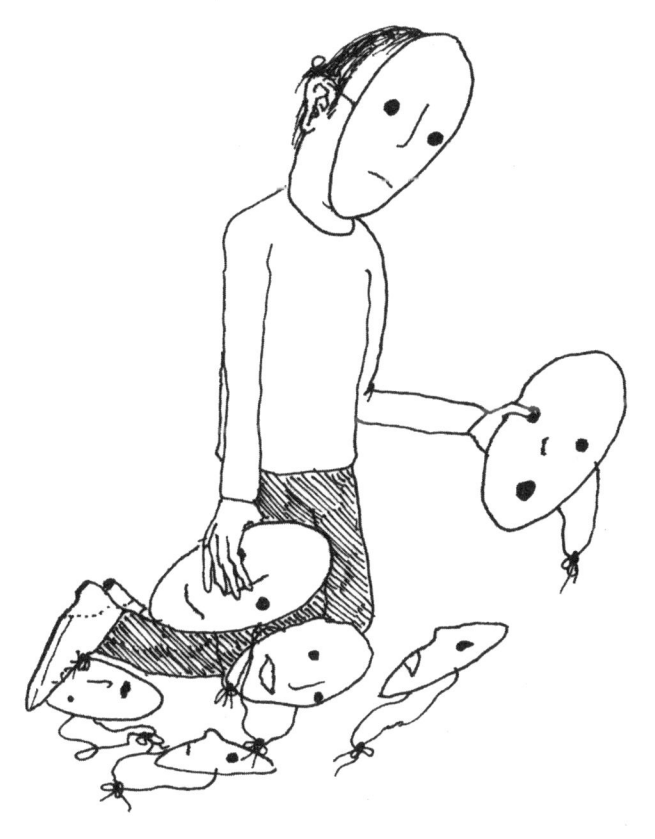

In late 1966, Brian Wilson, the Beach Boy genius, was working on a new album, titled *Smile*, which he described as "a teenage symphony to God." It was ambitious in every aspect, and as such it was an enormous undertaking. But just when Brian had spread all the puzzle pieces out on the table, the lights went out. His detractors crowded in, and his supporters were nowhere to be found. Brian already had a history of mental instability, and now he fell spiraling into doubt and paranoia. Finally, he abandoned *Smile*—hid it away in the dark. And then Brian hid as well—for almost thirty years.

But while he was lying in bed, picked-on kids everywhere were sitting in the sanctuary of their own rooms listening to Beach Boys records and dreaming of what *Smile* might be—hoping for Brian at a time when Brian had given up hope for himself.

In 1995 he remarried and, for maybe the first time ever, Brian felt secure. It wasn't long before he wanted to make music again. So he hired a new band. And they didn't just back him up—they carried him. While Brian stared blankly at the wall, they rehearsed and rehearsed in hopes that the music would coax his soul back into his body. They gathered all around him on the stage, stepping up to the mic whenever Brian grew too weary or worried to sing. In other words, they loved him.

But even with this new leaf turned over, *Smile* was still a dark chapter looming in Brian's past, and he was afraid to open it again. If anyone were to bring it up, Brian would say, "It's inappropriate music. I don't want to talk about it"—end of conversation. So loving Brian Wilson meant making room for his old anxieties; it meant setting places at the table for his unfriendly ghosts. But the new cast of Brian's story gave him that kind of grace every day.

So when Brian and his wife Melinda arrived at guitarist Scott Bennett's Christmas party in 2000, Scott invited Brian to just sit and play the piano for a bit. "We'll be in the other room," he said. "Join us when you're ready." So Brian sat down and the party began without him.

> And on the darkest night of the year,
> As the whole hemisphere
> Braced for another long winter,
> The most unexpected thing happened:
> After years of silence,
> First a melody, then
> A word.

And everyone rushed into the room to find Brian singing the opening bars of *Smile*, his voice like the voice of a child.

A Last Time For Everything

We're running out
Of fear and doubt;
We're low on loneliness.
And long goodbyes
Are in short supply.
We're coming to the bitter's end.

Tired of the letdowns,
'Cause they never let up,
When learning to do without
Is all that you ever get enough of.

Well, there is a last time for everything.

Then what of this earthly life?
It's a beating sustained
By a knot of nerves and veins—
A trembling choir.

We are born born to pass away
And nothing gold can stay;
I'm a dwindling fire.

The seasons spin around me
As I'm breathing in and out,
And ever my heart is pounding
A steady, unstoppable countdown

to the last time for everything.

You have to look death in the eye—
In the eye!
You need to see what's hidden there.
You need to see that he's afraid to die.

But you, my love—
You're gonna wake up soon
In your lonely room
To the sound of a singing bird

And throw the curtain back
To find your bag's already packed
And the cab is at the curb.

And, like a bad dream,
Unreal in the morning light—
So will the world seem
When you see it in the mirror for the last time.

'Cause there is a last time for everything.

Someday, somewhere in the world, a funeral will take place. It will be like any other funeral in every respect, save one: it will be the last one—ever. The mourners will weep, but their tears will be among the last ever shed in grief. The solemn pallbearers will not know that their steps are the final steps in a long procession ushering death out of our midst to be buried beneath the broken earth, inside that final casket.

And death shall be no more, neither shall there be mourning, nor crying, nor pain anymore, for the former things have passed away.
Revelation 21:4

I wrote "A Last Time for Everything" for Emmett Stallings after he was diagnosed with esophageal cancer in early 2010. He passed away in June of 2011. He was husband to Wendy, father to Quinn, a kind soul, and a faithful friend to many, including me. I asked Wendy if she would contribute something to this book, and I'm glad she did. I think it serves as a fitting benediction.

"For most of our life together the future stretched before us as incomprehensible as eternity, until one unexpected diagnosis collapsed that future into a steady, unstoppable countdown marching forward with relentless determination. People and seasons swirled around us in a flurry of empty activity, but all we could hear was the pounding of his heart as the unwelcome measure of his days. Our life together became one long, last goodbye to a world that had already left us behind."

"At the end, lying on our bed, I watched Emmett's chest rise and fall, holding my own breath to match his until I knew from the coldness of his skin that he had finally woken up from this bad dream—woken up to an eternity whose piercing light burned away the scars of fear and doubt leaving his skin all pink and new; where the songbird's melody broke his heart with the anticipation of a longing soon fulfilled; and where someone had loved him enough to buy his ticket and pack his bags. I imagine at the start of his journey that Emmett smiled in the mirror as this world faded away into unreality and eternity opened up before him."

ABOUT THE AUTHOR

The son of a scientist, Ben Shive was born in St. Louis, Missouri, where he grew up on a steady diet of Bible memory verses, 8-bit video games, and vinyl records. He moved to Nashville, Tennessee in 1999 to study composition and arranging at Belmont University. Just before graduating, he married his college sweetheart, Beth. Together they settled in a little house on the outskirts of Nashville, where they are currently quite busy chasing their four young children. Ben produces records at a little studio he calls the Beehive and travels the world playing songs with his good friends Andrew Peterson and Andy Gullahorn.

. . . .

ABOUT THE ILLUSTRATOR

Benji Anderson was born in Nashville, Tennessee in 1996. Growing up as the son of a graphic designer in Music City, he has been around art and music his entire, short life. When he is not attending high school, Benji practices piano, plays video games, and draws—and, truth be told, he often draws in class! Benji gave up countless hours he would have otherwise spent playing The Legend Of Zelda to produce the dozens of pen and ink drawings featured in this book and in the *Cymbal Crashing Clouds* CD packaging. Both attest to the triumph of Benji's pen over his ADD.